D1455836

Urban Woodland

Urban Woodland

A low-maintenance garden for Australian conditions

SUZANNE J. PRICE

Photography by Julie James

For those who would dare to break with traditional Australian gardening and create for themselves a haven of peace.

The urban woodland is the prettiest of all garden styles, providing an endless display with little maintenance required once established.

LOTHIAN PUBLISHING COMPANY
Melbourne   Sydney   Auckland

First published 1986
by Lothian Publishing Company Pty. Ltd.

© Suzanne Price 1986

National Library of Australia
Cataloguing-in-Publication Data:

Price, Suzanne J.
    The urban woodland.

    Includes index.
    ISBN 0 85091 255 2.

    1. Gardening — Australia. 2. Trees in cities —
Australia. I. Title.

635.9'77'0994

Designed by Derrick I. Stone Design
Typeset by Pro Comp Productions, South Australia
Printed in Singapore

This book is dedicated to all those who lost their gardens in the tragic Ash Wednesday bushfires of February 1983, when many of Australia's most beautiful gardens were destroyed. I hope that you can find the heart to re-create, perhaps not for yourselves but for future generations, another fine example of the living art of gardening, at which you are so skilled.

Suz Price
March, 1986

In all climatic zones, lawn
areas need to be lightly shaded
from November to April and
sunny for the rest of the year,
for the lawn will die out if it is
continually in shade.

FOREWORD

To speak of the Australian garden as if these words conjured up a clear image of a garden style, just as Japanese gardens or Italian gardens do, is clearly incorrect.

Two factors work against this broad view. Firstly post-settlement Australia has no cultural heritage on which to build. All of the world's garden styles build upon religious and cultural inheritances to establish a particular style related to that country. In Australia we are currently establishing the foundation upon which future generations can develop.

Secondly we must recognize the fact that Australia, while one country, is made up of many climate and soil zones. These tend to work against a single gardening style and encourage designers to create specific solutions for the environment within which they work.

Perhaps the answer is to develop an Australian garden philosophy, adaptable to all situations but following a single over-riding theme. This is exactly what is suggested in *The Urban Woodland* and how right it seems for the Australian environment, allowing us to enclose our cities in an envelope of foliage, improving our atmosphere, modifying our climate and providing both suburbs and rural areas with a continuous display.

The philosophy also suits our life styles since it permits us to reduce the time spent in garden maintenance and the use of artificial and sometimes damaging herbicides and fertilizers, and encourages the development of natural cycles within the garden system. Pools, outdoor-living areas and play spaces for children become magical openings of dappled light filled with the colour of flowers and foliage.

This image is not beyond any of us who follow Suzanne Price's suggestions. Yet, more important perhaps, is that we do not turn our back on any of our existing gardening precepts. Rather, we should design a garden in our normal way, establishing pictures to relate to our house so that we always enjoy seasonal colour groupings and effective planting schemes.

As the text points out, we attribute too much to flower colour in our gardens and not sufficient to the qualities of foliage colour and texture, or to trunks or fruit, or any of those qualities evident in our trees through the cycle of a year.

I welcome this excellent book as an addition to Australian horticultural literature for it offers stimulation to all who seek new solutions to the problem of Australian garden style. What I especially welcome is the fact that the overall style and philosophy is adaptable to both native-plant gardens and the so-called exotic-plant gardens. The division we have established in our mind between these gardens is as absurd as the author suggests.

I commend *The Urban Woodland* to all gardeners. It may not offer the solution to every garden problem but it certainly offers a direction for us all.

John Patrick
Victorian College
Agriculture and Horticulture
Burnley, Victoria

CONTENTS

PREFACE

Australia has found individuality in the arts and the sciences, and it is time we found it in gardening, which is both an art and a science. We are very well advanced in the science of horticulture, but in the art of gardening we either cling to English tradition or plant an all-native garden as if the rest of the world had nothing to offer. As we have done in other fields, we must take what is most suitable from the centuries of knowledge gained elsewhere, adapt it to our conditions and blend it with our own resources. This book presents a style which enables each gardener to do just that and points out how this is best achieved.

Gardeners in all areas could adapt this idea for their own use. Suitable climbers would ensure that the plants beneath were protected from heat or cold or tropical rain or salt-laden winds. What a pleasant stroll through the back garden.

The writing of a book, no matter how small, cannot be achieved without the help of others. I gratefully recall those who have been of assistance to me along the way, from the germ of an idea five years ago, through its gradual evolvement into the picture-planned cottage-woodland, until its realization in the form of this book. I cannot name all who have in some way been helpful, for such a list would surely include every friend and colleague with whom the project was discussed. I must, however, express my sincere thanks to those special people without whose help or encouragement I could not have succeeded:

- To my husband and three children for their patience and understanding, and for their encouragement whenever I faltered. I could not have completed this book without their support.
- To my sister Julie James who has spent four years photographing the desired aspect of each garden, skilfully capturing the scene or mood which I wished to portray. Our one regret is that we could rarely find a complete garden picture or a picture-planned garden which could be photographed to portray this essential ingredient of the urban woodland. Despite this, Julie's fine photographs are an inspiration for all potential urban woodlanders.
- To my dear friend Jenny Dimitriadis who for the last year has patiently typed and retyped the text, all the while encouraging me with her enthusiasm for the task.
- To my good friend Barney Hutton from whom I have learnt so much, not only about gardens and gardening, but about such mundane matters as sentence structure and syntax.
- To all those generous garden owners who have given us the opportunity to photograph their gardens, either by personal invitation or by opening their gardens to the public.
- To the anonymous people whose gardens have been photographed from the roadside, I thank you for beautifying our suburbs.

Suz Price

INTRODUCTION

In the beginning there was a garden.
It is thus a natural course for us to follow;
This striving to re-create the Garden of Eden.

The home garden began in this country as an attempt by early settlers to re-create the semiformal, or rather wild, gardens which had evolved around the cottages in English villages. These had no expanse of lawn, and any grassed areas were kept roughly trimmed by the animals living there. Water was not piped to garden taps, so the plants learned not to need it, and certainly conditions were conducive to the survival of hardy plants.

The English people have always been great collectors of the world's plants, and those plants which thrived in the manor garden generally found their way to each garden in the village. No great gardening skill was required. Snippets or seeds were put into the ground — if they died, they were considered unsuitable, and if they survived, they were appreciated but not pampered. Quite often the plants would seed themselves and pop up in a far more congenial spot and settle there.

Some of the early efforts to reproduce this type of garden in Australia were successful and such gardens can still be seen occasionally in the older suburbs, around old homesteads and in areas where conditions were suitable for the European plants that were used — such as in Tasmania and the hills near Sydney, Melbourne and Adelaide. But in many areas the conditions were too harsh for the type of plants used, and knowledge of southern-hemisphere plants was limited. The settlers had far greater non-gardening problems to cope with, and so, even in Melbourne where most of the plants brought from the old country would have succeeded if given protection from the north wind, this traditional-type of home garden was neglected. Gradually the suburban garden, as we know it, began to evolve.

I cannot understand why Australian gardens, particularly those in the suburbs, evolved the way they did. What has now become traditional is to have 'the front lawn', 'the back lawn' and gardens around the perimeter. This is the suburban stereotype, and what a dreary sameness it offers us!

In Australia the houses are set much further back from the street than in many countries. You would think that the reason for this is a wish for privacy or perhaps to escape from traffic noise. But do we then create a delightful garden to protect us from people and noise? Not very often. In general we keep this space as open as we can with an area of lawn, which is rarely used, and push our garden beds to the edges as if we are ashamed of them.

Of course there have always been some people who have delighted in surrounding themselves with beauty and have discovered in the process how little work there is in a well-planned garden. I thank them for breaking the monotony of our drives through the suburbs and country towns.

The purpose of this book is to pick up where the early settlers were forced, through lack of time, knowledge and the plants themselves, to give up, and to adapt their idea of the perfect home garden to suit Australian conditions. I have not attempted to state exactly which plants will grow where, for soil conditions and even climate can change from suburb to suburb within each city. As you discover what does grow and what should grow (and even what might grow) in your locality, this knowledge may be used in conjunction with the principles, methods and suggestions set out. The range of plants, both native and exotic, available today is so broad that anyone, in any part of Australia, will be able to create this type of garden for themselves.

Everyone can have a charming urban woodland, the prettiest of all garden styles, in which to enjoy a continuous display without continuous work.

Tree-cover need not be dense to supply an ample quantity of mulch each year. Little handling of the leaves is required, apart from raking paths and lawns and spreading leaves in places where they may have accumulated in deep piles.

ON THE STYLE

Create a garden after the style of your mind.
Whether it be tidy or wild, formal or natural,
Let it be a place for your enjoyment
and that of your children.

The type of garden which the first European residents tried to re-create was not always a garden style. It was something that happened over several hundred years, varying from house to house and from village to village according to growing conditions and the horticultural likes and dislikes of the owners. Now it becomes a style in our efforts to reproduce for ourselves the end product of those centuries of evolving gardens in a manner suitable for our conditions. It is not a stereotype style by any means. It is completely adaptable to any area, any type of house and size of property, and any specific requirements of the owner.

Adapting the old cottage garden style
In adapting the old cottage garden concept to suit Australia's harsher conditions, we firstly incorporate many evergreen shrubs, either native or exotic. These are used principally to insulate the garden from the hot drying wind. Secondly, we require deciduous trees to give the garden protection from the hotter sun. We use fewer perennials than there were in the old style, as a great number of them are sun-loving, but we have the advantage of being able to include more woodland plants, many of which I regard as the gems of the plant world.

This pretty autumn setting is suited to cool temperate areas. If another choice of trees was made, it could be used in warmer zones. A house immediately behind this planting would have privacy, cool summers and ample winter sun.

What we end up with is a totally new concept in garden design. I see it as a cross between the old English cottage garden and an area, still to be seen in some of England's grand old gardens, called the 'woodland garden'. Incidentally, the woodland garden has always been an area requiring less maintenance. This new style has many cottage garden attributes but, as the planting itself is closer to a woodland garden, I have called it the urban woodland.

Principles of the urban woodland style

I believe, as have some garden designers of the past, that a good garden, no matter how small, is not seen in a single sweep of the eyes. I therefore consider this to be the first principle of the urban woodland style. The garden must be segmented with each area giving glimpses of another, enticing you from one enchanting spot to the next. It is a parade of many different visual effects giving unexpected pleasure at the turning of every corner of its winding pathways. Thus it is a garden of separate pictures, each partially screened from the others, allowing the owners to incorporate any plants or group plantings they have seen, read of or dreamed about. This makes each urban woodland as different as the owners themselves. No two gardens need to be alike, expect in principle.

In the most attractive gardens there is no room for bare earth, so the second basic principle is that of covering every available piece of ground with something that grows. This of course cuts down on maintenance in the form of weeding. There will be times when some of the plants become dormant. This provides an opportunity for mulch to be applied, so that bare earth is not seen even above dormant bulbs.

The third design principle of the urban woodland style is that lawns are used only as play areas or for the purpose of opening up vistas— lawn maintenance is a tedious task. Those who seek the elusive 'maintenance-free' garden will learn that a well planned and planted garden is much less work than a lawn, and that open areas need not be planted with grass. You can have a thyme lawn, an alpine lawn or an area of low, spreading plants with stepping-stones between them.

In an urban woodland all edges and corners are softened by an overflow of plants so that no edge trimming or hedge clipping is required. A formal section can be incorporated into the garden if desired, but in general the softness of the design is the fourth principle.

A garden ought to be designed to blend with a house. The fifth design principle is that the house and its urban woodland garden together become the home. If a house has hard features, the garden should soften them. If it is a pretty house, plants should be chosen to accentuate this.

As a sixth principle I suggest that the urban woodland is not a static design. It is a garden that grows with you—as your ideas change, so the pictures within your garden change. You should always add to it or change it if you wish, because a garden must always suit the person who lives with it.

Surely the purpose of having a garden is for relaxation and enjoyment. Thus the seventh principle is that the urban woodland should require very little maintenance. If you feel like gardening you can find something to do, but if you don't, it doesn't matter.

If you design your garden with these seven principles in mind, and if you employ, where applicable, the methods and suggestions discussed later, you will have the pleasure and satisfaction of creating this prettiest of garden styles—the urban woodland.

For those who desire a rather wild approach to their houses, this type of woodland setting could become an intriguing front garden in most areas.

ON BEGINNINGS

A garden designed, created and cherished in harmony is surely a great bond between a man and a woman.

If you have just completed a house and are contemplating the garden, you are in an enviable position. Although there is a lot of ground work ahead, at least you can have a garden where everything is of your own choosing, designed for you or by you to suit your needs and desires.

Establishing a new garden
Your first job is to break up the soil. The easiest way is with a rotary hoe. Do not be tempted to break up the clumps and rake it immediately. Remove as many perennial weeds as possible, then leave it for a few weeks and go ahead with your planning. If you know or have been advised that the soil is poor, and you need to import some better soil, this must be spread over the rough-hoed ground and then hoed in with a rotary hoe. It is not wise to put a thin layer of imported soil on top of your local soil, as this creates a barrier which roots may have difficulty penetrating.

Where the soil is very good, there is no need even to hoe it, as any digging over upsets the balance of micro-organisms in the surface layer. However, I generally dig each new area of garden once, because it is easier to remove the perennial weeds from the looser soil. I do not spray because I am not yet convinced that even the non-residual herbicides are completely harmless to the friendly bacteria in soil.

Do not level out any natural mounds or depressions in your land. A mound helps to screen off an area quickly, so incorporate it in your plan, with one of your favourite pictures peeping out from behind it. A mound is also a good place for plants which require a drier position. Depressions can be utilized in the reverse way. Plan trees to shade your little valley, and you have an ideal spot for moisture-loving plants.

If this is your first garden, and you do not know where to start, purchase a good basic gardening book which includes a list of plants suitable for your area together with descriptions, height, width and flowering time. Then begin to study the area in which you live, and find out the names of any plants you see growing successfully that you would like to have. All gardeners love to talk about their plants and to give advice when asked. Find a good nursery where you can be given advice and possibly even plant lists for your area. If you wish, seek the services of a garden designer who is prepared to plan an urban woodland garden to suit your requirements. Do not have artificial landscaping done if you can avoid it, because this can be expensive and rarely looks natural, especially on a small block.

Think about your planning carefully. Even if you are having your garden designed for you, there are decisions you will have to make yourself. An urban woodland requires a large number of plants, but as many of them will be ground plants and bulbs, the cost need not be high. It does not cost as much to cover your land as it does to carpet your house, and the plants, if well-chosen, will outlive even the best carpet.

Converting an existing garden

If you have purchased a house that already has some garden, or if you have decided to convert an existing traditional garden into an urban woodland, your first job is to decide what to keep. You must discard any plants you don't really like, for you will never be happy with them in your new garden. Existing plants that are worth keeping can then form the basis of your plan.

This enchanting nook in a small suburban garden could be adapted for use in any climatic zone.

In shallow-front gardens such as this, the direct approach is sometimes the best. This perfectly straight path is nicely softened while still allowing easy access to the rear yard.

Good planning has ensured that the boundary fence, although it is only about a half a metre from the path, is completely screened. Notice also that branches are not intruding on the path, and that the scene changes from season to season.

ON PLANNING

*Plan in your youth a garden which will give
you contentment and satisfaction in old age.*

Most people find that it is a good idea to have a plan to work from. I use
a large sheet of paper in the shape of the land. The house, out-buildings
and any existing trees and shrubs that are being retained are shown in
scale on this sheet. I show the eventual circumference of trees with
dotted lines denoting that other plants can be used underneath, and
show the circumference of shrubs with solid lines.

Making a plan

Decide where your service area is to be. Make it just large enough for
the clothes-line, rubbish bins, compost bins, wood pile if you have a fire
and, if you desire, vegetable garden. Then plan to screen this area off
with quick-growing evergreen shrubs, those that will grow high enough
and thick enough to keep the wind off the vegetable garden, but not off
the clothes-line.

Mark on your plan where the sun rises and sets in winter and in
summer. In our southern latitudes this can vary considerably, and a
tree strategically placed to shield you from the late afternoon sun in
summer will not, even if evergreen, shut out the afternoon sun in
winter. If you use trees for protection from the midday summer sun,
make sure that they are deciduous so that they let the winter sun
through.

Using your knowledge of where the sun will be at all times in all
seasons, plan to shade your house from the hottest summer sun and to
capture as much winter sun as possible. Most houses are insulated from
within, but it is also possible to insulate from without. Medium-sized
deciduous trees are a great help, and evergreen shrubs against the walls
can keep out a good deal of summer heat and winter cold. If your area
suffers from a severe prevailing wind, plan a thick shrubbery to protect
your house and your garden from the worst effects of this.

Look closely at your house. Decide which features need disguising
and which you would like to accentuate. Anything you wish to hide,
whether a pipe, a hard corner or a large expanse of brickwork, is best
hidden by a broad-leafed evergreen shrub. Consult your list of suitable
shrubs and choose one which will not have to be cut away from a
window or path later on and thus have its shape spoiled. To highlight
an attractive feature of your house, such as a pretty window or a
shapely gable, choose a dainty-leafed tree or shrub and set it to one side
of the desirable feature. The eyes are automatically drawn away from
the solid green of broad-leaved shrubs toward a lighter, delicate-leaved
plant.

Decide where your open areas are to be, and whether they will be lawn or low shrubs. They may be for summer shade and winter sun, for opening up a vista of a distant section of garden or for catching a distant view. If your view is not a broad vista, but just an interesting outlook at one point only, it will be more effective if you frame it with trees or shrubs, as a photographer attempts to frame a photograph of a view. Plan for your living picture-frame to grow up in the appropriate place.

Planning your paths

Plan where the paths through your garden are going to be. Remember that a path must lead somewhere. In the urban woodland, paths tend to lead from one pretty setting to another. It is enough that the owner knows where they are leading and why. Trees may meet overhead along the paths, but make sure there is no encroachment of the paths by low branches or shrubs. It is a good idea to have a path underneath the wires bringing power and telephone to your home, then you won't be tempted to place a tree under them. Similarly, if the wires are underground, have a path above them so they will not be disturbed by the roots.

An enticing path such as this leads you on a pleasant stroll through the back garden.

The main paths, those which carry the heaviest traffic to and from doors, can be surfaced as soon as you begin the garden. Brick-paving or cobblestones will give a more natural look than concrete, and can be chosen to blend with your house. Don't be in a hurry to surface the other paths within your garden. Level them out, allow natural grasses to cover them and keep them mown. While your garden is young, weeds will tend to germinate in your paths and gravel paths can become untidy very quickly. Weeds in a grass path can simply be mowed down. Also it is much easier to change the width, shape or course of a grass path.

When the garden is planted and the positions of the paths are finalized, you may find that you like the look of the grass paths and decide to leave them. If they are to be gravelled, you will need to remove the grass in turfs about 8 cm thick. Level the new surface and put down a thin layer of sand. Next lay down weed-control mat which will allow drainage without any weed growth. Cover this with another thin layer of sand and then fill with the gravel of your choice. Granitic sand, although quite expensive, makes a firm surface immediately and requires little maintenance over the years. If weeds are allowed to go to

This long garden is nicely segmented with paths and peninsulas of shrubs, so that the whole is not seen at once.

seed in your garden, some will inevitably germinate in your paths but, by this time, your maintenance levels will be lower and young weeds are not difficult to remove from the gravel.

Even straight sections of path look natural when plants are softening the edges. Can you imagine this path leading through the beautiful pink and white display to the front door of your home?

Planning your pictures

Plan the segmentation of your garden to allow for glimpses of your various pictures as you wander from one to the other. A garden should not be seen in a single glance, but the segmentation must not be obvious. It must end up looking natural, so it requires a great deal of thought. This is where the advice of a garden designer can be a great help. You may also find that the example designs given in this book are useful as a guide. Use plants that you know to be successful in your area as the basis of your plan, then within this framework you will find that plants more suited to other areas can be given conditions conducive to survival.

Decide which glimpses of your garden you wish to see from each window of your house. It is pleasing if each window frames a different picture. If you wish to disguise your boundary fences, remember that after several years trees do not screen them; a tree trunk hides nothing. If some sections of your fence are screened with shrubs and some with creepers, interest is added and corners are provided for some of your pictures.

Dense shrub plantings such as this will hide boundary fences and give a garden a private, secluded atmosphere.

You are lucky if your land is not completely level. A little depression will hold extra moisture for plants that like water. A mound helps to partially screen off a portion of the garden. Any ups and downs add interest, so do not level them out. If you have a desire for a rock-garden, remember that many rock-plants like open positions and allow for this in your plan. Take advantage of a slope on which to construct a natural-looking rock outcrop. Mounds of rocks formed into rockeries never look natural.

If space permits, allow for a wild section of garden where rampant creepers may grow at will and forget-me-nots make a carpet of blue each year. Here you may have to push through a curtain of greenery to enter and experience the restfulness of your own secret garden.

Finally, begin to draw into your plan each of your favourite pictures, for this is where the charm of your urban woodland lies. If you do not have set ideas regarding which pictures you desire, start looking further afield to discover some. Botanical gardens can give you ideas, and private gardens which open occasionally to the public often have very charming settings. Some examples of pictures are included later in this book. Visit as many gardens as you can. This will be a great inspiration to you in the planning stage. Think back to the plants that attracted you as a child. If you are still not certain of exactly what you require, it is wise to leave a few spaces. One day you will know exactly what you want in a particular spot.

Once your plan is complete and the planting done, never feel that that is the end. Your garden grows with you and you change it as your ideas change. An urban woodland is as adaptable as you are and, of course, as the trees and shrubs increase in size, they provide conditions suitable for plants which could not be included in the beginning.

ON THE PICTURES

Work hand in hand with nature in your garden.
Apply your artistic eye to the plants which she provides,
For you will achieve in harmony
Beauty which neither could quite achieve alone.

What I am constantly referring to as a picture does not generally apply to just one plant in flower. It should be a pleasing group of plants providing a full picture. It may consist of a tree, with shrubs and ground plants underneath—all in bloom at once. It may be a mass of woodland gems blooming at the same time as a tree which frames the picture. It may be just a group of shrubs in a peninsula of your garden. The scope is unlimited, the only stipulation being that the plants in each picture must contribute to one another and to the picture as a whole.

If you choose to use just one type of plant for a picture, then mass it, but with restraint. If it is a shrub, plant at least three or four. If it is a bulb, plant dozens. The effect of a massed area of one plant can be good, but care must be taken not to overdo this type of planting, particularly with bright colours and bold foliage. Plants which I feel are often over-used in some areas of Australia are those with grey, silver and bluish foliage. Used thoughtfully, they are most effective. But they are generally plants of hot dry climates and, although we may think of grey and silver as 'cool' colours, planting an expanse of these plants (as a colleague of mine aptly put it recently) is a bit like creating a saltbush plain. There are many other plants which, like these, are better used in suitable pictures than in large groups or drifts. Even in a small garden there is scope for full pictures. It is better to have the year covered by seven or eight well-planned groupings than to have scattered plants in bloom or to have a complete display in one season and a dull garden for the rest of the year.

Choosing the colours

For the urban woodland to present a parade of visions which is both pleasing to the eye and satisfying to the mind, the experts would tell us that the colours used in each picture should be either harmonious or complementary. Harmonious colours are those that merge into each other in the rainbow, such as yellow, yellow-orange and orange, or violet, blue-violet and blue. Used for a more striking effect, complementary colours are those opposite to each other on a colour wheel, for example yellow and violet, or red and green.

Tints, which are any colours mixed with white, can be used in appropriate harmonious groupings, such as pink and mauve with violet and purple. Tints are best kept away from complementary groups, although this is often difficult as there are rarely pure primary colours. Shades are the base colours mixed with black. These and tones, which are colours mixed with both white and black, are already in existence in the browns of bark and the dark greens and greys of some foliage, and provide a sobering effect.

All this may sound theoretical, but if you trust your own instincts as far as colour schemes are concerned, you cannot go far wrong. If you think that certain colours look right together, then by all means use them together. It is your garden after all, and it must please you in all respects. Nature breaks all the rules and the effects are pleasing or striking. The colour schemes I prefer to use when planning pictures are pink and grey with a little white, burgundy and pink with some white, apricot and cream, soft yellow with cream and tan, and (where a more striking effect is desired) red and white, blue and gold, blue and white, and purple and gold. There are many other combinations which are worth experimenting with, according to your taste.

I should stress that the colours you choose to use must be pleasing to you, the garden owner. Although it is very pleasant to have others admire your garden, you have to live with it and work in it day after day, year in and year out. It does not matter if occasional visitors find your red and white picture too striking, or if your bold use of magenta and pink make them shudder. Taste in colour schemes is personal.

Gardening writers often describe pictures within their own gardens as examples of the use of colour. They are trying to pass on their knowledge and ideas, but unfortunately it is often their personal likes and dislikes that are remembered. The late Gertrude Jekyll did not like the colour magenta, or found it difficult to use in her favourite harmonious colour schemes. I think it a shame that her main legacy to gardeners, in Australia at least, has been a scorn of magenta flowers. Now that her books are again available, perhaps we will gain from her great knowledge and experience and be less influenced by her personal taste.

Vita Sackville-West wrote: '*Provided one does not run the idea to death*, and provided one has enough room, it is interesting to make a one-colour garden . . . There are two internal gardens of this sort *within* my own garden'. One of these, the white garden at Sissinghurst, has become the most imitated garden in the world. It is fashionable to plant gardens crammed with white flowers and as many grey- and silver-foliaged plants as possible. Some of these are successful for they depict the likes of their gentle owners, but to people who have a liking for colour in some degree, many are uninteresting and may even be depressing.

I think that if I had the space I would create a small white garden in a secluded area, as a retreat for reflection without the distraction of colour, but I would find it boring to look day after day at a white and grey scene which varied only by one white flower giving way to another. When I consider the wealth of wisdom which Vita Sackville-West imparted to gardeners, and her desire for us to show initiative, I am disappointed to think that she is remembered most for the white garden which she regarded merely as an amusing experiment. In her own words: 'There can be no rules, in so fluid and personal a pursuit . . . What this mass (of plants) shall consist of must depend . . . above all upon the taste of owner'.

A pretty spring picture of pale and deep pink suitable for Australia's cool gardens.

A blue and white summer picture at the front entrance gives way to a blaze of autumn colour from the trees overhead, which is complemented by the autumn tones of the hydrangeas themselves.

Choosing the plants

Just as plant colours come in and out of fashion, so do the plants themselves. It can become as confusing and as expensive to have a fashionable garden as it is to have fashionable clothes. You would be replanting the garden every year if you cared about following fashions. At the present time you would be filling your garden with old-fashioned roses and 'cottage-garden' plants, and possibly trying to do it all in white, which of course is not the way to depict a true cottage garden.

If you have just discovered the old-fashioned roses and have fallen for their many charms, then by all means include some in your garden. If it is an established garden, there is probably something you want to be rid of anyway. Cottage flowers, which I mention in another chapter, add a certain carefree atmosphere to any garden and, if you like some of them, use them. The point I am trying to make is that, as with your choice of colours, you should choose plants because you like them enough to live with them, and not merely because they are fashionable. Similarly, never buy a plant which you don't really like just because it seems to complete a picture—it is better to leave a space. Otherwise, temporarily use something cheap and easily removed, for you will sooner or later find a plant which you do like and which is right for the picture.

When planning the pictures for your garden, think carefully about your use of trees and shrubs which have the capability of featuring more than once during the year, for example those which have spring flowers and autumn-colour foliage. You may be able to position them between two pictures so that they feature when in flower with a grouping on one side and when in colour with a grouping on the other.

A harmony of pink shades provided by cherry blossom, rhododendrons and azaleas, made all the more pleasing by the touch of pale blue of forget-me-nots.

Viewed from the other side, the flowers are thrown into sharper relief and the shadows are more intriguing.

Another alternative is to have the ground plants under the tree included in the spring picture, while the plants around or on either side would feature in the autumn. However you go about it, you can plan to get the maximum benefit out of each plant. Similar care must be taken with plants such as the Lenten rose (*Helleborus orientalis*) and the winter iris (*Iris unguicularis*) which flower for six months, continuing to bloom long after the other plants in their pictures have finished. If the groupings round about them are suitable, these lovely winter flowers can also be used in spring pictures.

Pattern of pictures

If you are planning to have more than one picture featuring at a time, or to have pictures which will overlap in the season of their display, separate them with a grouping of plants which will flower in another season. This will save a possible clashing of colours and will also add interest to your garden.

Another alternative is to have a 'progressive picture', where one colour scheme is chosen for a section of garden, and plants of these colours flower progressively during a period of many months. A progressive picture in my garden is pink and white, beginning in August with *Prunus campanulata* and *Rhododendron* 'Cilpinense' backed by *Viburnum tinus* with *Helleborus niger* (the true Christmas or winter rose) underneath. The viburnum and helleborus continue flowering for months, while other prunuses and rhododendrons come and go. The picture is completed in early December with *Kalmia latifolia* and a late-flowering azalea (its name not known to me) which has a low, compact habit of growth and many large pink flowers. Plants within this progressive picture do overlap in their flowering times, but this does not matters as their colours blend into the chosen scheme.

Using perfumed plants

Proceed with caution when using perfumed plants. It is wonderful to have perfume in your garden at all times, but the scents must be in harmony. Two strong perfumes together can overpower each other (and you), some can overpower gentler fragrances, and some simply do not blend. If you are not sure whether certain scents will be suitable together, it is wise to separate them. You will still be able to have a perfumed plant in each picture, for the pictures themselves are separated.

Blooming in sequence

Care must be taken to choose the right variety of each plant, for if a mistake is made a plant will bloom out of sequence with the rest of the planting in the picture. For example, you may see a grouping which you love, consisting of a tree with white blossom above dark red rhododendrons interspersed with white azaleas. You must find out what the tree is, for white blossom can occur from July until October. Even finding out that the tree is a flowering cherry is not enough, for the different varieties bloom in sequence for almost three months. You need to know the name of the specific variety which will flower for several weeks in the chosen setting. Then you must find out which particular rhododendron and azalea complete the picture, for the flowering time of this genus extends from June until December, with each variety in flower for several weeks within that time.

This same problem can arise with any plant belonging to a large genus. There are acacias and eucalypts in flower at all times of the year, and even daffodils have a season of seven to eight months. If it is possible you should identify the plants when you see them flowering together. An alternative is to let an expert plan each setting for you, or at least have as a guide a gardening book which is specific about flowering times or lists group plantings. The list of suggested pictures included in this book may be of some value if the plants are suitable for your locality.

Flowers and fruit can be combined to create interesting and unusual pictures. In the example shown here year-round interest is also provided by the contrasting foliage.

Natural rock formations can enhance pictures, as this warm temperate garden reveals.

Even these methods may not be a success. You may see two plants in bloom together only to discover later that one was finishing its season and the other beginning. A shower of rain in your district can cause some plants to bloom earlier than in an area which did not get the rain. Thus seeing two plants in bloom at the same time in adjacent suburbs may not be an accurate guide. A higher altitude will delay flowering time, as will a shadier aspect.

A safe method of ensuring concurrent flowering in your pictures, and in fact a method I have used with some success in designing pictures for gardens in unfamiliar areas, is to select a plant with a long flowering period as a companion for one with a short season. For example, knowing that *Viburnum tinus* flowers all winter and into spring, you can confidently place any early-flowering blossom with it and be ensured of success.

Competing plants

If you desire to use a plant which has the reputation of being a garden robber, you should choose its neighbours carefully, or you could lose half of your picture in one season. For example, acanthus provides excellent foliage contrasts with its huge, glossy, dark-green leaves and its flowers are useful in summer pictures, but it will quickly gobble up 2 metres of garden, smothering better-mannered plants in the process.

But you can 'set a thief to catch a thief' with very good effect. I have surrounded the silverest of silver-leaved shrubs, *Chrysanthemum ptarmicaeflorum*, which spreads and sprawls in many gardens, with

White and gold are good partners for picture planning. Where no better mulch is available, straw may be used, and in this instance it blends quite well with the colour scheme.

A more distant view of the same garden reveals that the plants on both sides of the above setting blend nicely with it. The introduction of a small amount of soft mauve provides an interesting finishing touch.

acanthus, in this case *A. spinosus*. These jostle each other in their struggle for superiority, choking all weeds in the process, and provide a stunning foliage effect. The chrysanthemum has never looked so silvery-white as it does against the glossy, dark green acanthus leaves. Their summer flowers coincide and are good together, but are merely incidental in this planting. In another area I have *Matricaria eximia* 'Golden Moss' (dwarf golden feverfew) and *Anthemis biebersteini* competing to take over the front row of a long garden bed. The gold and silver tapestry thus produced is quite beautiful. Here again the flowering is good but incidental—merely a reminder that good pictures do not need to rely only on flowers.

Be prepared to change

I hope that all these points and warnings do not make the task of picture-planning seem daunting. I am really trying to prepare you so that you do not expect to get every picture right at the first attempt. Be prepared to shift plants about until you achieve the desired effect. Treat the prettying up of your grounds as you would the furnishing of your house, where you shift the furniture at will until you are satisfied. Small plants are easy to move and resettle in their new position. Larger ones are more difficult, but not impossible.

You will find that it is the smallest plants, the finishing touches, which need the most readjusting until you are pleased with their siting. Some people will then leave the garden pictures for as long as they are in residence. Others may decide after some years that a change is needed, and rearrange the pictures or add new ones. Your garden is as versatile as you are, particularly where smaller plants are concerned.

ON COTTAGE PICTURES

Let a flower grow where it will,
For in the wild and unplanned garden,
Nature is the greatest artist of all.

There is one more type of pictorial effect which I must mention here, even though there are books devoted entirely to it—the 'cottage garden' planting. A riot of mixed colours is produced by mass plantings of hardy shrubs, perennials, self-seeding annuals and bulbs. No serious consideration is given to colour schemes, and if colour clashes occur, as they occasionally must, these are blurred or hidden within the overall floriferous gaiety.

The cottage picture must seem to spontaneously emerge, as in fact it often did in the cottage gardens of English villages. The effect is best achieved if there are no straight rows of plants, no careful groupings, no neat edging plants and no obvious colour co-ordination. Even height is not a consideration. If your cottage picture can have a little path winding through it, part of its charm will lie in the fact that small plants, which could not be seen from the front, can be discovered among the taller plants.

Cottage flowers blooming with gay abandon in a small suburban front garden. This early summer scene affords great pleasure for people passing by.

Planning a cottage picture

If your garden is large enough for a section to be planted in wild abandon of this type, may I suggest that you aim for mid-summer or even a little later to be the peak of its delights. This can be a rather dull time in even a well-planned garden unless you fiddle each year with summer-flowering annuals or take on the high-maintenance task of a herbaceous border featuring at this time.

The area involved should not be heavily shaded, because the plants you will use require some sun to produce their best effect. Small-growing, small-leafed trees which have a light, informal habit of growth are most suitable. Flowering cherries cast dense shade, but most of the other blossom trees are satisfactory. These will of course flower earlier, perhaps in sequence with shrubs which create a wind-break and backdrop for your cottage picture. Japanese maples are ideal, but it may be necessary to remove their lower branches to allow headroom for your cottage flowers. Fruit trees are also good, and are very appropriate as they are often seen in the old cottage gardens in England, along with elder trees (*Sambucus nigra*) and guelder roses (*Viburnum opulus*).

The range of shrubs suitable for this type of picture is quite extensive. They could include the shrub roses which bloom in mid-summer. Some of the escallonias would be good, along with abelia, daisy bushes of many types and (of course) lavender. Alternatively, the shrubs used could be the lilacs, camellias or rhododendrons which have featured earlier in their own picture. These can now be wreathed with summer-flowering clematis species, light-growing climbing roses or even sweet peas. These climbers would be cut down during an autumn clean-up, which would also include the cutting down of perennials and the removal of spent annuals.

There are numerous bulbs and perennials which are suitable for a cottage picture, and many of these are becoming available in Australia. I cannot mention them all, but will recommend a few which do flower in summer. Perennial asters and campanulas should be included, and any perpetual-flowering corydalis which you can obtain. Lilies, colchicums, alliums and heuchera are available, and lavender showers (*Thalictrum* spp.) and perennial peas (*Lathyrus latifolius*) can at times be obtained. Further inspiration will come from visiting gardens, particularly old ones, and good nurseries during summer.

The old-fashioned annuals and biennials which are to be used in this type of picture are not always readily available. The best method at present of obtaining these true cottage flowers is to beg seed of them whenever and wherever you happen upon them. Most gardeners are happy to share their treasures in this way, and you will find that where these plants have become established, the owners have more than enough for their own needs. Some that I suggest you seek are love-in-a-mist, Californian poppies, *Viola cornuta*, hollyhocks and honesty, the latter flowering in spring but then producing shining silver discs (seed pods) which last all through summer. Easily obtained annuals which may reproduce themselves in your garden are sweet william, godetia and candytuft. When removing the annuals at the end of their season,

This late-summer cottage effect is well suited to the hotter, more arid regions as well as warm temperate places.

shake their seed about to ensure that they repeat their pretty display in the following summer.

To achieve a cottage picture, you need not set aside a special area. I would suggest another method which I intend to try myself. The garden should be carefully picture-planned to provide beautiful displays one after another for ten months of the year. Cottage flowers could be interspersed through all the pictures so that suddenly, at about Christmas time, the whole garden would burst into a blaze of colour. Even for areas of quite dense shade, there are some summer-flowering perennials and self-seeding annuals such as viola species, some of the campanulas, the mallows and bergamots, which could make the picture complete. The autumn clean-up would ensure that the winter sun streamed through, enabling the bulbs and other little gems to successfully perform once again in their own picture.

Self-seeding annuals such as forget-me-nots can be used to provide a cottage garden effect in spring as well.

Two views of a one-year-old cottage garden in summer. Many young trees and shrubs have been planted to provide flowers and autumn colour, and in winter and early spring choice bulbs make an excellent show. But it is these annual and perennial cottage flowers which provide an air of gay abandon for months in summer and early autumn.

ON PICTURE-PLANNING

*The gardener-artist works with living
colours, shapes and textures to create
a mobile tapestry of wondrous beauty.*

When the plan of your garden has reached the stage where it shows the
basic layout, with all buildings and proposed buildings, service and
outdoor living areas, paths, outlines of trees and shrub peninsulas
marked on it, you will be ready to begin your picture-planning. Now is
the time to allocate space for each picture and to design each one
separately. Always work within the limitations you have set for yourself
on the plan, such as the sizes of the trees which will form the framework
of your garden and the positions of the paths which will make each area
accessible and manageable.

Making adjustments
As you proceed with the picture-planning, you may find that some
adjustments to the plan are necessary. Perhaps a picture will be screened
more effectively if the shape or size of a shrub grouping is altered. A
certain favourite picture may require a larger area. A path may need a
little more curve to be alluring, or it may need to widen out at a certain
point to allow for an extra seating area from which to view a picture. A
large area of garden may need a small track through it as a short cut
between paths, to make maintenance easier or simply to divide two
pictures.

Such things are minor adjustments and are to be expected, especially
if this is your first garden design. But, before making any major
change, think back to your reason for the original siting. A spur of the
moment decision now could cause you to lose a view, block a drain,
obstruct a path, screen out winter sun or let in the summer sun. After
consideration, if you decide that your reason for the change is valid and
that the garden will be better for it, draw it into your plan and proceed
with the picture-planning.

Building the pictures
Many of your pictures will be easy to design, as they will consist of your
favourite plants or of groupings you have seen. But, if you are not
immediately sure of a complete picture, it is a good idea to begin by
choosing the tree which will grow to the size shown on your plan, and
then build up a suitable picture around and beneath it.

It may be helpful at this stage if I take you step-by-step through one
of my own picture-planning experiences. The plants which I used will
not be suitable for all areas, but it may be useful to know the procedure.
The picture-planned section of garden discussed here is an area
contained by the front boundary, a side boundary, the driveway and a
path which gives access to a neighbouring property. It needed to be

screened on the two boundaries to give privacy and to provide a
backdrop for the pictures. The front boundary already had a heavy
screen of mixed evergreen shrubs and small trees. These I left for the
time being. A young golden elm was also left. All other plants were
removed. The basic plan (Figure 1) showed that two extra trees could
be used.

The picture-planning began with the need to shift a tree to make way
for an extension to the house. The expected dimensions of this tree,
Prunus serrulata 'Shirotae' or 'Mt Fuji', were right for the area involved,
so it was carefully sited and planted. Next I considered what to plant
under it. There are several azaleas which are suitable, and a drift of
bluebells would be lovely. In another garden I have used *Lamium
maculatum*, which works well. But, in this instance, I chose
Rhododendron 'Florence Mann' which produces a mass of violet-blue
flowers. Thirteen plants of this small-growing rhododendron were
sited in their pots and studied carefully.

At this point it is necessary to view the area from all angles while
picturing in your mind the eventual size and shape of the plants. Move
the pots about until you are quite satisfied with their siting, for a few

The purple form of weeping
Japanese maple (*Acer palmatum*
var. *dissectum Atropurpureum*)
is highlighted by its green
counterpart and enhanced by
the flowers of the shrubs
nearby.

Figure 1

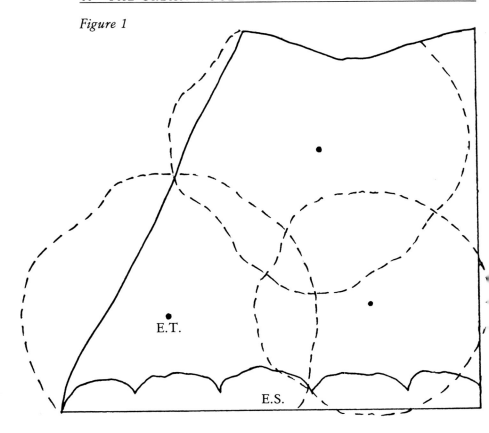

E.T.

E.S.

extra minutes spent now may save you shifting established plants at a later date.

Not very long after being planted, quite a few of these rhododendrons began to die. On inspection, I discovered that they had been set too deep at their last repotting. Depth of planting is always important, and with some plants it is critical, so remember to plant no deeper than the existing soil level (always trusting that the nursery has it right) and keep dense mulch away from the stems. A mulch of leaves, whether applied naturally or artificially, does not seem to cause any problems.

After replacing all the victims, unfortunately with smaller plants, and extending this planting by adding several more of the same rhododendron, I proceeded to the next step. As this is a small-leafed plant and quite upright in habit, enough light penetrates to allow for another layer of planting. I used *Anemone nemorosa* var. *bracteata*, the double, white wood anemone, to create a white carpet beneath some of the rhododendrons. The soil was mulched, and thus the first picture for this section of garden was completed (Figure 2). It is not perfect every year, for the cherry has the habit of blooming well every second year, and in the year between has fewer flowers which do not last very long. It must be kept free of low branches or the rhododendrons closest to the trunk do not receive enough light to flower well. However, when this picture works well, as luckily it did in its first year, it provides inspiration for the creation of more such works of art.

Figure 2

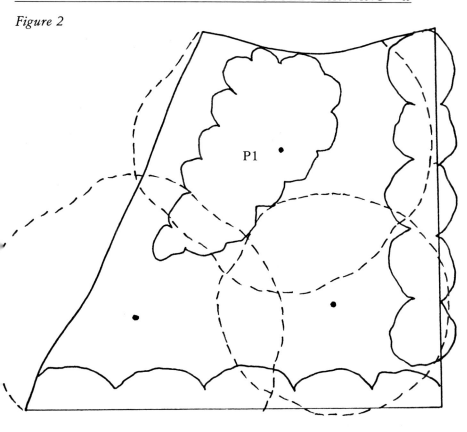

Before proceeding with my picture-planning of this area, I made notes about the finished section. I strongly recommend that at the completion of the planting of every picture you write down the name, preferably the correct botanical name, of every plant used. Even the best of memories cannot be trusted to retain a string of unfamiliar names, and plant labels stuck in the ground not only look unsightly but fade or snap very quickly. By the time your urban woodland is complete you will have planted many hundreds of plants, and could not be expected to remember the correct name of each one. But, if you get into the habit of naming each plant correctly, you will gradually become as familiar with such names as rhodohypoxis and oxydendron as you are with rhododendron and oxalis. Referring to your plan from time to time will help you to gain this familiarity. I am not suggesting that you write every name directly onto your plan. It is a better idea to number each picture on the plan and to list the plants of each picture separately, thus allowing for changes to be noted without the plan becoming a mess.

The next step in my picture-planning was to plant a row of *Nandina domestica* var. *nana* along the driveway edge of the garden bed. These are now meeting up to become a low, informal hedge which is a strong feature throughout the winter. This edge is raised due to the cutting-in of the drive, and the soil is held by a line of large rocks. Between the nandinas, I planted *Erysimum pulchellum* to flow down the rocks to a narrow strip of soil at their base. Here *Sternbergia lutea*, the lily of the field, enjoys the dry exposure and the warmth reflected from the rocks. In their separate seasons the flowers of both the erysimums and the sternbergias are highlighted by the colourful foliage of the nandinas.

I next chose and planted *Pieris japonica* 'Bert Chandler' as the background shrubs along the side boundary. This is a favourite shrub of mine, providing year-round interest with its foliage, which is pink as new growth, becoming cream and finally pale green. As a bonus this shrub has sprays of lily-of-the-valley-like flowers in late winter and early spring. It is quite a dense shrub, well-furnished with foliage right to the ground. I thought that these pierises would be good companions for the next picture to be planted in this area. I do not regard either the foreground planting of nandinas or the background shrubs as pictures in their own right, but rather as secondary incidents to provide interest when the complete pictures are out of bloom (Figure 3).

For the second picture I chose *Rhododendron* 'Alice' and *R.* 'Loder's White'. The former is quite a tall-growing rhododendron with large conical trusses of rich pink. It has the habit of becoming rather bare and leggy underneath. *R.* 'Loder's White' is the perfect companion for planting in front of *R.* 'Alice', as it is shorter and has a tendency to spread gracefully. The flowers are large and white with a wavy edge of pink when first open.

The grouping of these two plants alone created a picture, but as there was space for a tree to give the flowers some protection from the November sun, I selected *Prunus serrulata* 'Shimitsu Sakura'. This is the last of the cherry blossoms to flower, and in my opinion the loveliest. It makes a smaller tree than most, with large, semi-double blooms hanging in graceful clusters from long stalks. They are pink in bud, opening to become pure white. I have not yet planted this tree as I have only been able to find specimens which are grafted as high standards. I do not like the artificial habit of growth thus created. I would much prefer to allow a tree to form its natural shape and then prune it a little if necessary, so I am prepared to wait for this one.

I was recently given some seedlings of white forget-me-nots which I planted among the rhododendrons. If these naturalize I will remove the earliest seedlings each year so that the later ones, thus given extra space and light, will flower at the same time as the rhododendrons. This can be practised with any self-sown annuals and biennials. As they germinate over quite a long period, they will flower for an equally long time provided that the earlier ones do not smother the later, smaller ones. If you can be bothered fiddling with them, you can time their flowering to fit in with appropriate pictures.

As this second picture came into bloom for the first time, my first disaster in picture-planning became painfully obvious. The new growth on the pierises, which I had remembered as being pink, was quite salmon next to *Rhododendron* 'Alice', which in turn revealed a mauvish tint in the pink flowers. The clash was horrendous, and the five pierises were hurriedly removed to form a peninsula elsewhere in the garden. I now realized that even had their new growth not clashed with the rhododendron's flowers, it would still have detracted from them. After

Rhododendron 'Alice' and *R.* 'Loder's White' combine well in this late spring picture.

Figure 3

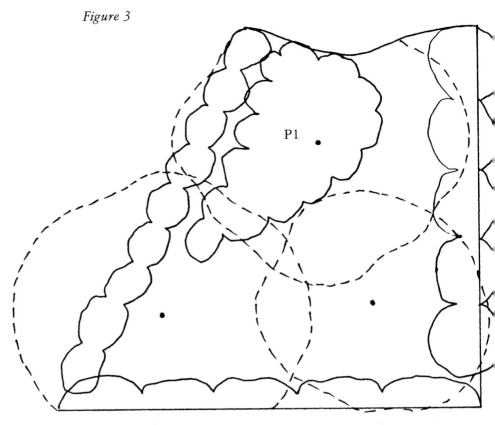

some consideration, *Dodonaea viscosa* 'Purpurea' (purple hopbush) was used. Its bronze-purple foliage shows the flowers of *R.* 'Alice' up nicely, while at the same time the size and shape of these bushes will create the required screen.

The other disappointment in this picture came with the realization that one of the rhododendrons purchased as *R.* 'Loder's White' was in fact *R.* 'Mrs E. C. Stirling'. The .flowers of pink became pale mauve and, although lovely, detracted from the picture. This shrub was removed and another *R.* 'Loder's White' purchased. This was not the only occasion on which I have bought incorrectly-named plants, and I feel that it is incumbent upon growers to take care in naming their plants. The retail nursery person and the garden owner depend upon the grower to be accurate, and many could show a more professional approach.

With two pictures completed except for the late-flowering cherry and all the tree and shrub space allotted (Figure 4), I now considered the use of bulbs and perennials to create another display in this garden bed. I decided to use lilies and to plant them among the small rhododendrons and nandinas, for they like to have their bulbs and roots in the shade and push up through protective foliage to flower in the sun. I selected, when in flower, mid-century hybrid liliums in colours ranging from pale lemon through yellow, gold and apricot to deep orange. Finally I planted, in any available spaces, seedlings of *Oenothera*

Figure 4

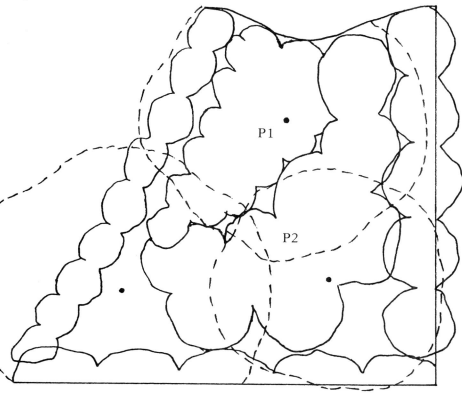

biennis, the biennial evening primrose. It fortunately doesn't wait until evening to open its bright yellow flowers, which it produces continually for many months.

Finally, the whole area was mulched, notes were taken, and this picture-planned garden bed was completed. This does not necessarily mean that it will remain as described. Already white forget-me-nots and white dicentra have been added, and I have planted *Schizostylis coccinea* (Kaffir lily) to push its spikes of scarlet flowers up through the nandinas in March. I intend to plant the cream-flowered *Zephyranthes* x 'Ajax' among the sternbergias, and *Euphorbia myrsinites* to replace some of the erysimums. The existing screen at the front will be replaced with purple hopbushes. If the 'Florence Mann' rhododendrons fail again I will not replace them, but will use something else. The oenotheras are too tall among the lilies so next year I will replace them with *Mimulus lutea*, the yellow monkey flower. I hope that any necessary or preferred changes will not involve the trees and large shrubs, but I think that flexibility with the smaller plants is necessary for good picture-planning. As your skill develops and your confidence increases you will gain much pleasure from improving each of your living works of art.

Maintenance

Two years after completion, this garden bed, which covers about 35 square metres, had reached the stage where six hours each year were spent on maintenance. This maintenance time is becoming less each year and I expect that it will have halved by the time the trees and shrubs have met and intermingled. The whole area is weeded and mulched in autumn before the lilies drop their seeds, which then fall and germinate in the mulch. In this way the lilies are naturalizing and as old bulbs die from exhaustion, young ones will be ready to flower. I have no intention of lifting, dividing and generally cultivating in such a heavily planted area. I do make the one concession of occasionally giving the lily clumps a top-dressing of good compost, for they are plants of rich soils and repay such attention with vigorous growth and abundant blooms.

In late winter there are usually a few weeds and other unwanted seedlings to be removed and sometimes a little pruning is required. This is completed before the lilies begin to emerge and while the oenotheras are still small enough to step between. This is also the time for the top-dressing of compost if it happens to be available. In summer a pleasant evening is spent removing any weeds which may have germinated during the spring.

Judging success

This is one of the first areas of my garden to be seen upon entering, and the picture-planning has ensured that it provides a nice welcome all year round. In January and February the lilies and oenotheras feature. By March the nandinas are colouring respectably, highlighting the yellow oenotheras. These continue right through the autumn while the nandinas get brighter and brighter above the golden chalises of the sternbergias, and the golden elm and the cherry take on their autumn tints. Even after leaf-fall the oenotheras produce scattered flowers until finally they finish in mid-winter. Now the nandinas appear even more brilliant beneath leaden skies, and the erysimums begin to produce their pale yellow flowers. The 'Florence Mann' rhododendrons assume their winter dress of bronze foliage. These and the large rhododendrons provide substance beneath the skeletons of the trees. During late winter and early spring the colour of the nandinas begins to soften and lighten as some of the scarlet leaves become apricot and yellow. Below them the erysimums are smothered with flowers, and the outline of the trees above soften as their buds break forth. By October the nandinas, although still colourful, have mellowed to the point where they do not detract from the lovely sight of the white cherry and its companions. Right through November the rhododendrons 'Alice' and 'Loder's White' flower, and during December the lilies once again begin to bloom.

Because picture-planning is an art rather than a science, I am unable to set down rules which you might follow in order to create a picture. Instead I can only hope that this brief description of one of my designs and its results may provide some inspiration for other gardeners wondering how to begin.

A simple yet effective picture, not quite at its peak in this photograph, where marigolds accentuate the beautiful foliage of *Gleditsia triacanthos* 'Sunburst', which is further highlighted by the dark green of the background trees and shrubs.

PICTURE YOUR
GARDEN YEAR

Every day of the year
A flower will smile at you
and at its companions in harmonious beauty.

Having described the planning of garden pictures and the difficulties involved in getting them right, I thought it appropriate to describe some of my favourite pictures. Those I have chosen feature in succession throughout the year, ensuring at least one good picture at all times. These pictures are suitable for most areas of Tasmania, south-eastern Victoria and New South Wales, the hills of Sydney and Adelaide and with some adjustments could be used in certain areas of Queensland and Western Australia.

Summer

A striking picture for December is one which I chanced upon in my garden. Without realizing that they would flower together, I put *Sandersonia aurantiaca* at the rear of a planter box and *Lotus bertholettii* to flow over the edge and down the front. Sandersonia is the Christmas bells of South Africa—a tuberous plant with a winter dormancy needing a very well-drained position. It has 0·5 to 1 metre leafy stems, sometimes semi-twining. From the leaf axils hang urn-shaped bells, 2 cm wide, which are the colour of a ripe mandarin. The lotus is a trailing plant with fine, grey foliage and large pea-shaped flowers of scarlet tipped with yellowish-orange. It must have protection from frost, but is otherwise very easy. I would not have thought of combining the colours of these two flowers, but they do create a pleasing effect, both in the garden and in the house as a Christmas decoration.

During January a lovely picture is provided by white hydrangeas interplanted with hostas in the background and bletillas to the front. The large, often-variegated foliage of hostas is always attractive in a shady spot (providing that snails are controlled) and is effective as a weed-smothering ground cover. The tall spikes of pendant, mauve, bell-shaped flowers are lovely among the hydrangeas. *Hosta lancifolia* and *H. fortunei* are generally available, and for a taller spike of deeper mauve flowers, *H. ventricosa* is worth seeking out. I like to mass *Bletilla striata* (Chinese ground orchid) in the foreground, where its spikes of mauve cattleya-like blooms complete the picture.

One of my favourite garden pictures is the carpet of pink and white created by interplanting *Cyclamen hederifolium* with *Leucojum autumnale*. The latter is the autumn snowflake, which from a small bulb sends up several 15 cm spikes each having one or two dainty white bells edged with pink. The cyclamen, previously known as *C. neopolitanum*, has pretty, reflexed flowers 10 cm high, usually in varying shades of pink though sometimes white. It flowers from the beginning of February until mid-June, while its silver-marbled, ivy-shaped leaves are an attractive ground cover from the end of March until December. During February both of these plants are flowering without their leaves, making a most unusual display. This effect can be achieved in sun or shade, but these plants do seem to colonize more readily in the mulch under deciduous trees.

Autumn

In early autumn a most attractive picture can be achieved in a sheltered, elevated garden bed or in a large tub using a pure white fuchsia such as 'White King' (several if space is available) planted with *Gentiana sino-ornata* (the Chinese ornate gentian). This is a fine-leaved trailing or mat-forming plant which has large trumpets of very deep blue striped with green. It dislikes light, sandy soils, and it must not dry out. If the fuchsia is tip-pruned during the summer, and if the gentian has shelter but not too much shade, both will be a mass of flowers in March, providing a blue and white effect that is hard to better.

A beautiful pink picture for mid-autumn can be achieved by planting a group of *Euonymus alatus* (the winged spindle bush from Japan). This is a medium-sized deciduous shrub with narrow, dark green leaves which deepen to burgundy and then turn bright pink. At the same time it is covered with pods which split open to reveal bright orange seeds; a startling contrast to the pink leaves. Underneath the spindle bushes should be massed with *Nerine filifolia*, a dainty, dwarf nerine with frilly flowers of a very deep pink, and fine, grass-like foliage which is often evergreen. If space allows it, this picture is even better if it is arranged under a claret ash (Fraxinus oxycarpa 'Raywoodii'). In April its deep burgundy foliage highlights the pink leaves and flowers.

Coming into bloom during May is a hardy crocus from the Mediterranean region, *C. serotinus* var. *salzmannii*, which multiplies freely in moderate regions and flowers profusely provided that it is kept fairly dry in January and February. The flowers are large and of a delicate lilac shade, while the throat is deep yellow. It is available during summer from specialist growers who advertize in garden magazines. This crocus is particularly lovely massed beneath *Betula papyrifera* (the canoe birch or paper birch), a tall, slender tree with bark which is much whiter than that of the silver birch, and larger leaves which turn to a rich yellow and stay on the tree for weeks. These serve to highlight the yellow throat of the crocus.

Winter

June can be a dreary month in an unplanned garden. It is important to have some pictures that will feature when the last of the autumn colour has faded and the deciduous trees and shrubs are bare. A very cheerful sight is the earliest of the winter-flowering daffodils, a treasure of the *Narcissus bulbocodium* group called *N. cantabricus*, still sold by specialist growers under its former name of *N. bulbocodium foliosus*. It is an elegant, milky-white hoop petticoat daffodil liking a sunny position which is dry in summer. It is very pretty when planted among *Oxalis hirta* var. *rosea*, a non-invasive oxalis with large, saucer-shaped flowers of vivid pink, and soft, fern-like foliage which makes a dense cover beneath the daffodils.

July can also be a dull month, and I like to brighten it with a grouping of the earliest blossom, *Prunus mume* (the flowering apricot). This only grows to about 2·5 metres and has perfumed flowers in white and various shades of pink. Among these, I plant several *Rhododendron* 'Christmas Cheer', which is the first to flower of the 'cool-climate' rhododendrons. It has a low, compact habit of growth and many smallish pink trusses of bloom. As a ground cover to complete this picture, I mass *Cyclamen coum*, which carpets the ground with shining, heart-shaped leaves of deep green and dots the carpet with its sweet, dumpy flowers in varying shades from white to the deepest pink.

In August a wonderful sight is a massed planting of *Primula vulgaris* (the English primrose) and *Crocus tommasinianus*. The primrose has creamy-yellow flowers with a golden eye and a delicate, sweet perfume. Planted beneath a deciduous tree, and not allowed to dry out in summer, it will multiply and cover the ground completely with its crinkly, pale green leaves, providing an interesting contrast to the leaves of the crocus, which are narrow and dark green with a central stripe of silver. *Crocus tommasinianus* is the easiest to obtain and the easiest to grow well of all the crocuses. It quickly establishes to form a large colony which will have hundreds of silvery-mauve flowers with golden anthers and styles. A massed display of these two plants provides a cream and mauve woodland picture worthy of a place in any garden.

Spring

Spring is a colourful season in most gardens, but the colour can be more effectively used if thought is given to planning for pictorial groupings. The queen of the blossoms, *Prunus serrulata* 'Shirotae' or 'Mt Fuji' is widely planted, but rarely is it seen in a picture which will enhance its beauty. As described earlier, I have underplanted mine with a group of *Rhododendron* 'Florence Mann', a small, narrow-growing, very free-flowering rhododendron. Its flower is similar to the much used *R.* 'Blue Diamond', but it flowers a week or two earlier and, to my mind, has a better colour. It is a vibrant violet-blue which seems to have an inner radiance of its own, and the effect of it massed beneath the white cherry blossom is quite superb. This is a picture which I look forward to in anticipation for the other eleven months of the year.

A little later in spring there is another of my favourite pictures. I have massed deciduous azaleas (*Rhododendron molle* and others) in varying shades from cream through apricot and salmon to orange, carefully avoiding the pinks and the more strident bright oranges and scarlets. As an evergreen backdrop for this picture I use *R.* 'Unique', a hardy rhododendron with a compact habit to 1·5 metres. It has medium-sized trusses which are apricot in bud opening to cream. This shows up the deciduous azaleas perfectly.

By November the main flush of spring colour is over, but your garden can still have a beautiful feature. *Laburnum* x *watereri* 'Vossii' (golden chain tree) is at its best. This is a small-growing deciduous tree which has long pendant chains of golden flowers. It can be espaliered or trained over a framework to create a tunnel effect. The latter is probably the most effective way to use this versatile little tree. As a ground cover I like to mass *Convallaria majalis*, lily of the valley, for its spikes of perfumed, creamy-white bells are open at the same time. If a little more height is required, *Polygonatum multiflorum* (Solomon's seal) is also very effective, with its gracefully arching stems of white bells tipped with green.

Foliage is as important as flowers in the creation of a satisfying picture. Ferns are charming against the bold foliage of camellias. This combination is successful in both cool and warm areas.

Sharply contrasting colours, such as the crimson and white of this setting, are softened by the greens, browns and greys around them.

NATIVES IN PICTURES

Every natural plant has a native home,
But not one is native to the artificial
environment of a garden.

Cultivating native plants

Every species of plant is a native of somewhere on this planet and, as such, is worthy of preserving. A great number of plants, from many different countries, are endangered in the wild, and it is a wish of mine that every gardener would give a home to at least one endangered species. All plants can at least be preserved in cultivation. The survival of many plants would also be fostered if each gardener would choose species rather than cultivars when buying plants.

Plant collectors of the past have done a wonderful job in carefully collecting plants from the wild and bringing them into cultivation. This has in fact saved some species from complete extinction as they have disappeared from their native habitats for one reason or another, usually encroaching civilization or over-zealous collection by amateurs. But, over the years, many species have also disappeared from cultivation because plant breeders like to feel they can improve on nature and, in the course of breeding, cross-breeding and interbreeding to produce something bigger, brighter or in some way better, have lost track of what they started with.

As the cultivation of Australian native plants is in its early stages, comparatively, there is the opportunity of not losing any species of plant. But, as I see grevillea flowers becoming larger, melaleuca bushes becoming more compact and in fact most natives in cultivation being in some way 'improved', I wonder about the fate of these species. Plant breeders will continue to produce so-called 'improved' cultivars, and growers will continue to mass produce them as long as gardeners will buy them, so I am glad that the current trend seems to be back to species. To meet this new demand, growers will propagate species of all kinds of plants and these will have the chance to survive in cultivation if not in the wild.

Australian natives versus exotics

When Australian native plants became popular, about 30 years ago, they were introduced in a way which led many people to believe that these fascinating plants could not be grown with exotic plants. Thus there developed two schools of Australian gardeners; those who had native gardens and spurned all other plants, and those who grew exotics and thought that natives would not grow with them.

Gardeners in the tropics did not become so divided, for they could see from the beginning that tropical plants from Australia and abroad would grow together quite happily. For gardeners in the south it was

not so simple. By habit many people were still watering nightly and feeding regularly, and this was not appreciated by the dry-area natives, which were the ones most readily available. Now, as gardens become more natural with less artificial watering and feeding, and with a wider range of natives from which to choose, gardeners in all areas are able to experiment with interesting blendings of natives and exotics.

But, as Australia is so vast with many climatic regions and soil zones, we should be trained to think of native plants in terms of which part of Australia is their habitat rather than just as 'natives'. Nursery staff could be more helpful too. They generally group all Australian

Native ferns are often used in woodland settings, blending very well with exotics. They also provide a contrast of foliage in such settings.

plants together so that the buyer has no idea of the origin and requirements of each. The 'grow native' propaganda has encouraged this, and
has also led many people to believe that natives are easier to grow than
exotics. This is not necessarily so. The term exotic is misleading. In the
horticultural sense here, it simply means any plant which is not
Australian.

Planting to suit conditions
The misconception that natives are easier has led to many failures. The
only natives easy to grow in any area are those indigenous to that
region or to a similar region in another state. Many people in the south-
east of Australia, for example, choose the colourful, profusely-flowering
natives of the south-west, which of course grow without trouble in
Perth gardens. These are taken from their sandy soil, excellent drainage,
dry atmosphere and very sunny conditions, and often give disappointing
results in clays or loams with damp conditions. Wherever in this large
country you may be, limit yourself to native plants from your own or a
climatically similar area. If you live in the east or south-east of Australia
and want to experiment with some of the glorious dry climate natives
of south-western Australia or elsewhere, be prepared to make special
beds for them, to water not at all (if you are a waterer) and to lose a few
each year and have to start again. Remember, native doesn't mean easy.

Exotic plants imported from somewhere in the world where conditions are similar will be less trouble to grow than unsuitable natives.
The former include not only the familiar large street trees, but also
small trees, shrubs, ground covers, alpines and bulbs. Some of the
easiest plants to grow in Melbourne, for example, are not natives.
Purple hopbush, variegated pittosporum, red photinia, hebe, diosma
and cotoneaster are just a few of the commonly-grown exotic shrubs.
Of the trees, birch, ash, elm, liquidambar, many prunuses and some
maples grow with ease, and most of the perennials, rock-plants and
bulbs are also exotic.

Planting to attract birds
These exotics all blend very nicely with local natives, and many also
have the great advantage of attracting native birds. In fact, in my
former garden, many birds including various honeyeaters, spinebills,
thornbills, silver-eyes, rosellas and wattlebirds fed all year round on
such exotic plants as fuchsias, camellias, prunuses, crataegus berries,
birch catkins and many more. The versatile little fuchsia, *F. magellanica*,
flowering virtually all year, seemed to be the staple diet of the eastern
spinebills. The wattlebirds were very fond of camellias, particularly
'The Czar'.

In my present garden, regardless of the inclusion of acacias, grevilleas,
melaleucas and various other Australian plants, many of the birds show
a marked preference for the imported plants. The silver-eyes love the
cotoneaster berries, the rosellas enjoy birch catkins, and the various
prunuses are popular. There are many other examples, but the highlight
of winter for the honey-eating birds is *Clematis nepaulensis*. The
greenish-cream bells with protruding maroon stamens are firm enough

to withstand the buffeting of wattlebirds, spinebills and three types of honeyeaters all feeding together for three months. Then, these remarkable flowers become large fluffy seed pods, just in time to provide a soft lining for nests. This hardy, fast-growing climber, which is deciduous for a short time in *summer*, is situated where I can see it and the birds from the winter sunroom, and it provides as much pleasure as any other plant in this garden.

Thus it is not necessary to grow native plants in order to attract native birds. It stands to reason that nectar-producing flowers should attract birds that love nectar regardless of where the flower originated, and to a seed-feeding bird a berry is a berry, whatever its botanical name. My garden is also well-endowed with insect-eating birds because I never use insecticides. These may not be actually harmful to the birds themselves, but they certainly deplete the food supply. Each gardener must make a choice between an abundance of birds and perfect blooms and foliage, for no matter how healthy plants may be, there will be times of insect infestation on both indigenous and imported plants.

Some broad-leafed exotic plants would add substance and the interest of foliage contrast to this predominantly native setting.

Combining natives and exotics

As we all become more confident about the mixing of natives and exotics, fine pictures will be developed. I am able to suggest some combinations which I know to be successful, and some which I feel

This wattle, both in bloom and out of bloom, provides a contrasting backdrop for the exotic plants growing near it.

would work very well. I have grown the New South Wales waratah (*Telopea speciosissima*) and the golden chain tree (*Laburnum* x *watereri* 'Vossii') side by side with stunning results in mid- to late-spring. The brown boronia (*B. megastigma*) is excellent in an otherwise cream or pale gold picture, and is lovely with a petticoat of *Narcissus* 'Silver Chimes'. I have admired year after year a Cootamundra wattle (*Acacia baileyana*) looking charming with a drift of snowflakes (*Leucojum aestivum*) beneath it. Recently I saw a late-winter-early-spring picture consisting of the green of *Euphorbia wulfenii* flanked by the orange *Correa reflexa*.

I feel sure that the New South Wales Christmas-bush (*Ceratopetalum gummiferum*), which is suitable for a variety of climates, could be used effectively in summer pictures. Even with such traditional garden features as the herbaceous border, native plants can be used. For a blue and white summer border, the native bluebell (*Wahlenbergia*

gloriosa) would make an excellent edging plant. Some of the lovely native alpine plants are becoming available and should grow well in conditions which suit alpines from other countries. Ground-cover plants such as the native violets are effective and are useful as cover above bulbs.

The same wattle becomes the 'light at the end of the tunnel' when approached along the path.

If you are uncertain as to whether the natives and exotics selected for a picture will combine successfully, be guided by the climate of their place of origin. Dry-climate grevilleas, for example, should grow well with plants from such areas as California, the south-west cape of South Africa and the countries around the Mediterranean. Natives of cool and mountainous regions combine with plants from the cool zones of Europe, New Zealand, North America, China and Japan. Subtropical east-coast plants are suitable in pictures with natives of Florida, the eastern cape of South Africa, and parts of South America.

However you use natives in your urban woodland, do not expect them all to be faster growing than your other plants. Some which are fast-growing, such as acacias, are 'pioneer' species. They are usually also short-lived, springing up rapidly after fires, protecting the slower-growing permanent species while they establish, then dying out when their task is complete. Otherwise, natives in general do not grow very fast in their natural habitats or under natural conditions. As with most plants, they will often grow faster in garden conditions with extra feeding and watering. Quite often plants which are forced to grow faster will die earlier because their life cycle is completed sooner. Pruning can extend their life, but what is the purpose of forcing quick growth and then cutting it off? It is better to let all your plants set their own pace of growth, and not to be disappointed if your natives are not fast-growing under these conditions.

Most important of all, never feel bound to plant only Australian natives because you are Australian. What you *ought* to plant in the garden is what you like, for a garden is a private affair. A discerning gardener will choose a plant which is suitable for the position and blends with the picture being created, regardless of its native land. After all, why should a plant be spurned because it is not a 'dinkum Aussie'?

If you were to visit a beautiful garden in England, you would not expect to see only British native plants in it. What you would see, and what you can have yourself, is (literally) a world of plants.

ON TREES

A year in the life of a tree is but a day;
The new growth of the spring morning
Is strengthened in the summer afternoon, and
Matures in the autumn evening.
Throughout the long winter night the tree sleeps,
Its roots wrapped in a warm blanket of yesterday's
leaves.

Gardens in Australia require more trees than are generally seen in the gardens around cottages in England. The climate is, in most areas, harsher in summer and autumn, so the gardens require more shade from the sun and shelter from the hot wind. Plants that are able to grow in full sun in Europe and the northern states of America often require some shade in Australia. When choosing plants described in English gardening books, remember that generally our winters are milder and our summers hotter, so make adjustments accordingly.

Trees form the framework of the garden as a whole and they also serve to frame or feature in many of the individual pictures. They can provide flowers or blossom, autumn colour, berries and winter effects as well as shade, mulch and protection for the whole garden. Careful consideration must therefore be given to the choice of trees.

The young trees in this garden are emerging to create a framework within which the rest of the garden will develop. Peninsulas of evergreen shrubs will provide substance in winter.

Selecting trees

Deciduous trees are far more useful than evergreen trees within the urban woodland, for each tree can also provide a variety of foliage effects and conditions. From the silhouette of bare branches against a winter sky, to the springtime promise and excitement of plump buds bursting into tender young leaves, to the lush greens of maturity in the heavy heat of summer and the gradual transformation to radiance in the crisp autumn air, a deciduous tree changes to suit the mood of each season.

The choice of deciduous trees for cool and temperate areas is very wide, with more rare and unusual species becoming available all the time. Gardeners in a subtropical climate can choose from such trees as *Diospyros* species (the persimmons), *Prunus persica* (flowering peach) and *Sapium sebiferum* (the tallow tree), to name but a few. For hot dry areas *Cercis siliquastrum*, *Gleditsia triacanthos* and *Koelreuteria paniculata* are among those which will succeed.

If you want any evergreen trees in your garden, make sure that they are small-growing ones. Evergreen trees cut out winter sun from a very large area and do not provide usable mulch. I have elsewhere discussed large-growing eucalypts and you must also be wary of the conifers that will grow large, particularly pines and cypresses. There are very few small plants that will survive under them and you could end up with a large, barren area in your garden. The scope provided by a large property is needed to accommodate them.

A good maxim to go by when selecting trees is never to plant on a suburban block any tree that will exceed 10 metres when fully grown. There are many to choose from that are smaller than this. Also remember that most trees have a spread of at least two-thirds their height, and that many have a width equal to or even greater than their height. You should consider this from the start, for trees that are too closely planted turn your garden into a forest where each tree cannot be viewed individually in its season.

Planning for trees

Consider your neighbours when you are planning for trees. Do not plant them on your boundary lines unless they will grow no more than 5 metres high, as they will block out your neighbour's sun either in the morning or in the afternoon, depending on the situation of your land. If they are evergreen they could block out all winter sun from an adjacent property to the south of you. Their roots will spread far beyond your boundary and will compete with your neighbour's plants for available food and water.

In any case, trees are not needed on your boundary. Most of them when grown are ineffective as a screen. A tree trunk does not hide a fence and the loose and open tops of many trees do not effectively screen your view of a neighbouring roof. The exceptions are those small-growing trees which grow like shrubs; for example the variegated pittosporum which remains thickly covered to the ground to screen a fence and does not open out at the top to reveal a roofline.

Thus keep trees towards the centre of your property. They will be

more use to you there, providing mulch as well as shade for woodland plants. In planning areas of urban woodland, aim for deciduous trees to meet when fully grown. If you are planning an area of lawn surrounded by a shrubbery, have tall shrubs at the rear of the shrubbery, graduating to the lower ones at the front. Towards the foreground have small-growing deciduous trees. Many beautiful plants will thrive under their dappled shade. These trees can also be placed so that they throw some light shade onto your lawn (if you must have one) in summer.

If you can avoid it, do not stake any tree. Staking has the effect of encouraging thin extension growth without the normal secondary thickening. Also a tree does not make for itself a strong enough root system if it cannot sway with the wind. The root system will also be too small for the size of a tree that has been forced into lush top growth with water or feed. Allow your garden to set its own pace; to establish a rate of growth which is suitable for the conditions.

Choosing the planting

Plant a tree for what it will give you. You may desire spring blossom above bulbs, or you may want a splash of autumn colour. Always consider what each tree will offer as well as shade and mulch, and when it will look its best. Some trees cast dense shade and only real shade-lovers may be planted beneath them, many of which will flower during winter and early spring while the sunlight can filter through the bare branches onto them, and then hide themselves away in the shade again for the summer. Other trees cast lighter shade allowing dappled sunlight through. Under these you can have a wide range of plants; in fact any except the sun-lovers from the desert fringes or the true alpines.

It is important to establish your plants, whether they be shrubs, ground cover, bulbs or perennials, under and around your trees right from the start if possible or at least within several years. The root system of a tree will be at least equal to the spread of its branches, and can even be several times more extensive. Once this is established it is more difficult to achieve a massed-planting effect. You may have to choose more robust plants than you desire for the spot. If all the planting is done when the tree is young, both the tree and its neighbours adapt to the shared conditions, and smaller-growing gems have a good hold before the competition becomes too great.

ON EUCALYPTS

Tall and stately in the forests let them stand,
These symbols of our ancient native land.

The eucalypt is essentially a tree of forests, either dense or sparse, or of open scrub land. Of the hundreds of species in the genus, only a very few have been tamed for garden use in suburbs. These few are worth having if you have the space, but there are many other native trees equally suitable and certainly much tidier.

The litter continually dropped by eucalypts is acceptable to the plants which naturally grow under them in the forests, but unfortunately not all of these are suitable garden plants. You may have noticed that in general there is only a good cover of plants beneath eucalypts in high rainfall areas, and that in the forests of the drier areas the lower strata plants are few and far between. This is natural and effective in the dry schlerophyll forests, but is not the look that most people want for a garden.

Eucalypts in the garden

To achieve a thick planting beneath eucalypts, you must be prepared to apply vast amounts of water because, although they do not require it for normal growth, the trees will absorb all the available moisture. The artificial watering applied to maintain the shrubs will keep the eucalypt roots close to the surface where they will then take all the nourishment required by the shrubs. This too will need to be replaced artificially. Even then, with high maintenance levels of watering and feeding, the desired effect may not be achieved.

In the forests, the tap root of a eucalypt will reach down to a great depth in search of water. This anchors it well. In a garden situation, especially where huge amounts of water are applied to maintain plants beneath the tree, the tap root has no need to be deep. The watering and also the feeding, which is used to compensate for what the eucalypt takes from the shrubs, has the tendency to create lush top growth quickly. The tree reaches the height where it catches the full strength of the prevailing wind, but is not anchored securely enough for its weight. The result of course is that it simply blows over, as seen so often with the widely-planted *Eucalyptus nicholii*.

This can also happen without the extra water. A young eucalypt will normally compensate for wind by anchoring itself sideways with extra roots. In cases where the tree has been staked or protected from wind by a fence or other screen, it may blow over when it outgrows the protection and is hit by the wind. A great many eucalypts when large also have the tendency to drop huge branches, which makes them dangerous for planting near people and houses.

It is wise to take great care, or seek good advice, when choosing eucalypts for your garden. Alternatively, try some of the small-growing wattles, which are just as appropriate, patriotically speaking. Many are far more suitable as garden trees although, as previously mentioned, many are pioneer species, and some do have the tendency to blow over after a few years, especially if watered incorrectly.

The place for eucalypts

You need not feel guilty if you don't have a eucalypt on your property. In most countries there are forest trees which are too large or otherwise unsuitable for garden use, and these are looked upon with national pride in the place where they should be—the forests.

The remaining forests and scrub lands should be saved, and replanting should be carried out where applicable. However, once such an area is subdivided and the land sold, the ecological balance is destroyed. It cannot be saved by refusing to allow people to remove eucalypts, which present a real hazard to life and property, from around their homes. Governments and local councils, having allowed people to build their homes in these areas, must then allow them to remove forest trees from their properties. By all means suggest that these be replaced with trees suitable for garden use, but it is folly to try to keep as forest that which is no longer forest but a residential area. Eucalypts which look quite safe now will need to be removed at great expense some years hence when they begin to drop limbs on people and houses. Conservation cannot be carried to the extreme whereby it infringes on the rights of individuals to protect their family and home.

Where eucalypts exist as a backdrop, safely away from the house, they are a good foil for flowers and foliage within the garden.

Footnote: In the aftermath of the tragic Ash Wednesday fires of February 1983, I add another reason for people to be allowed to remove eucalypts from their properties. Although due to the severity of the 'fire storms' in some areas, towns may have been swept by the fires no matter what was planted in the gardens, I am certain that the litter under the eucalypts and the combustibility of the eucalyptus oil in the leaves were the cause of many homes being destroyed. There are also many homes standing because their gardens of exotic trees and shrubs were slow to burn. These plants absorbed the heat and sparks and gave out their moisture which cooled the fire, slowed it and in some cases diverted it.

ON SHRUBS

Endow your garden well with shrubs,
Evergreen for substance and protection
And deciduous for life-giving mulch,
For each also contributes the beauty of flowers,
foliage and shape
To a garden of quality.

Shrubs have many uses in the urban woodland. They may feature in the pictures created, or provide a backdrop for them. They hide fences, service area, adjacent houses and any undesirable features of your house. They give protection from winds, both hot and cold. They serve to screen off certain sections of the garden, giving protection to plants beyond and partially hiding these until their time has come to feature in a picture.

Selecting shrubs

When choosing shrubs, remember that they take up more garden space than trees. The only planting space used by a deciduous tree is its trunk, and although a tree may be tall and wide, all the space beneath its branches can be used for planting. Shrubs, particularly evergreen ones, use up as much space as their width. Find out how wide each shrub will grow and keep in mind that, although you may plant something next to it to enjoy for several years, when the shrub has grown fully there will be no space or light beneath it for other plants.

Gardeners in warm and sub-tropical areas are able to experiment with bold groupings such as this, based on foliage effects with flowers playing a secondary role.

You may choose a shrub for the part it will play in a picture which includes also a tree and small plants, or you may select a group of shrubs which make a picture themselves, giving way to a later show provided by the little gems growing in the lee of the shrubs.

Shrubs which will grow to 3 metres tall or even less will create an effective privacy screen and wind-break. They will hide the service area without keeping sun or wind off the clothes-line. Shrubs that will grow to 4 metres will also hide a neighbouring roofline from a suburban yard, for as you look up to the top of the shrubs your line of sight extends above the roof. To hide an adjacent roof or a distant ugliness from your window outlook or from a raised terrace or patio, you may need to plant one carefully chosen larger-growing shrub or a small evergreen tree. For screening, it is a good idea to choose shrubs or trees that will grow no higher than actually required, for then you allow maximum winter sun into your garden.

When selecting these background shrubs, choose them also for winter effect. This can be achieved either by flowers or foliage. They are then a perfect foil in winter for the deciduous trees and shrubs growing in front of them. You do not notice the bare branches because you are presented with a new picture which was only partly visible from October until May. I am not implying here that deciduous trees are ugly in winter. Many are quite beautiful, and all are lovely after rain when the sunlight glistens on droplets of water quivering on every twig. Each tree seems to be studded with diamonds.

Consider shrubs also when choosing autumn-foliage plants. If you have a small block of land with space for only a few trees you can still have a blaze of autumn colour in all its various shades, for there are many shrubs to choose from which colour beautifully in autumn. Most of these also flower in another season, so do not overlook that fact when planning your features. Each section of your garden can provide a picture more than once in a year.

If you have room to do so, it is more effective to plant low-growing shrubs, such as azaleas, in groups rather than singly. This level of your picture then becomes a mass of colour, rather than patches of several colours. If the plants in your groups of these low-growing shrubs are close enough to intermingle after several years, they then provide excellent ground cover, for virtually no weeds will grow up through them.

Use medium-growing shrubs to create the peninsulas in your garden around which the paths will wander. This prevents the whole garden from being seen in one glance and provides the twists and turns in the paths whereby the visitor comes upon unexpected vistas and the owner upon anticipated pleasures.

Variegated plants, either evergreen or deciduous, can be put to good use to lighten dark corners or to highlight other plants growing near them. This idea can be developed under any climatic condition.

An effective use of shrubs for summer colour.

Shrubs play a predominant role in this spring picture.

These shrubs which screen a boundary fence emerge in a pictorial role in winter.

ON BULBS AND PERENNIALS

They never cease to surprise and delight,
These magical gems which children adore;
Hiding out of sight when conditions aren't right,
Then emerging from the earth to bloom once more.

From time to time throughout this book I have used the term 'ground plants', referring to all plants which are not trees, shrubs or climbers. Many of your ground plants will be perennials, either evergreen or herbaceous, and what I loosely call bulbs or bulbous plants. The latter may be bulbs, corms, rhizomes or tubers.

Shade requirements

A large number of bulbs and some perennials are shade-loving in their native habitats, which makes them natural choices for inclusion in the urban woodland. Wood anemones (*Anemone nemorosa*) are among my favourites, for their thin rhizomes spread rapidly beneath the mulch and the delicate-looking leaves and flowers create a delightful carpet. English primroses (*Primula vulgaris*) produce their sweetly-perfumed, pale yellow flowers all winter and spring in a moist, shady position. Snowdrops (*Galanthus nivalis*) and snowflakes (*Leucojum aestivum*) are a joyous reminder that spring is on the way, and bluebells, both English (*Hyacinthoides non-scripta*) and Spanish (*H. hispanica*), cast a violet haze over a stretch of woodland just as the new leaves are unfolding overhead.

Many bulbs and perennials which are classed as sun-loving really prefer to live in the dappled shade of deciduous trees when planted in Australia, for here hotter summers are the general rule. Many species of iris and colchicum are good examples. The latter is the 'meadow saffron' of Europe, often sold under the erroneous and misleading name of 'autumn crocus'. Even some of the nerines and crocuses become woodland plants provided that they are not watered in summer.

There are also some which, although preferring a sunny position even in the heat, will still grow and flower successfully in semi-shade. Many perennials fall into this category, along with bulbous plants such as belladonna lilies (*Amaryllis belladonna*), gladiolus species, vallota lilies (now *Cyrtanthus purpureus*) and some of the narcissus species. Admittedly many will not flower as prolifically, but in shade the substance of a flower is enhanced, and each flower will be longer-lasting.

Thus the scope of bulbs and perennials suitable for the lowest level of each urban woodland picture is extensive. However they should not be selected indiscriminately, for in an established woodland garden there are varying degrees of shade, and these ground plants must therefore be considered according to their shade requirements.

Under a canopy of large-leaved or dense-growing trees, such as oaks and some of the magnolias and ashes, very little light will penetrate in

Irises of many types may be grown among trees and shrubs, but do choose colours which will complement each other if flowering times coincide.

the growing season. Only the real shade-lovers are happy under these conditions. The Lenten rose (*Helleborus orientalis*) is the perfect occupant of such a position, for not only does it flower continuously from June until October, but it is virtually evergreen, providing excellent ground cover with its large, handsome leaves. The various hostas are also suitable. Their bold foliage provides wonderful contrasts in shade, shape and texture to other plants in their vicinity, and the golden-leaved and variegated forms will lighten any dark corner. In summer, as an added bonus, they send up spikes of delicate, pendant bells. Although they are not evergreen, the large leaves do smother the ground for much of the active growing season of weeds.

Beneath groups of finer-leaved or open-growing trees, such as Japanese maples, silver birches and many of the blossom trees, the shade is broken by splashes of sunlight. This is dappled shade and is the natural home of many treasured woodland plants. Apart from those mentioned at the beginning of this chapter, which are of European origin, I am delighted to say that some of the beautiful woodland gems of North America, such as erythroniums and trilliums, are gradually becoming available here and are worth seeking out.

In areas where trees do not meet overhead, or where an open area merges with woodland, there is shade, either dense or dappled, for part of the day and sun for the rest of the day. These situations require ground plants which are equally happy in either sun or shade. Luckily there are many bulbs and perennials which are suitable, for while the garden is young there will be more sun than shade, and as it matures this situation will gradually reverse. The dwarf, hardy cyclamens are most useful in these areas, as in fact they are anywhere in an urban woodland. If you purchase *Cyclamen hederfolium* for autumn flowers and *C. coum* for winter, and, soon to be available, *C. persicum* for spring and *C. purpurascens* for summer, you will have masses of these sweet, dumpy flowers all year round. The beautiful, glossy leaves are very variable, many having attractive silver marbling or margins. These provide dense cover from March until December, or in the case of *C. purpurascens*, all year round. They will do well in such extreme conditions as a hot sunny rock-garden or among the hungry roots of beech trees or conifers, but they will naturalize best where the seed falls into cool leaf mould.

A North American woodlander, *Erythronium tuolumnense*, which revels in dappled shade and cool conditions.

Ornithogalum nutans is easy
to grow, for it flowers well in
sun or it naturalizes in shady
woodland conditions despite
frosts, drought and heat.

The leaf mould is provided by the annual falling of leaves which have completed their brief role in the cycle of a plant. In early autumn deciduous trees and shrubs prepare for dormancy by converting the chlorophyll in their leaves into sugars and absorbing these, some of which are in turn converted into starch, which ripens the wood and keeps the growth and flower buds of next season plump and healthy. Many of these plants have a higher sugar content than is required to be absorbed. It is these surplus sugars remaining in the leaves which take on the brilliant shades. It always amazes me that this mundane chemical process can create such beauty.

Bulbs and perennials for each season

As the leaves fall, mulching the ground anew, the light is able to stream through. Now many woodland plants, particularly bulbs, awake from their own dormancy and start into growth. During winter and spring they grow, flower and seed, completing their cycle in early summer when the new leaves have grown to full size on the trees and shrubs overhead.

Thus are the cycles of plants. When deciduous trees and shrubs are in growth and are requiring the available nutrients and moisture, the bulbous plants beneath them are dormant and require nothing. When the latter emerge and begin to grow again, they do not have to compete for food and water with the trees and shrubs, for the roots of these are now inactive.

Winter- and spring-growing bulbous and herbaceous plants are therefore most suitable for use beneath deciduous trees and shrubs, particularly in areas with dry summers. In planning a garden picture which perhaps includes a beautiful tree with a background of shrubs, bulbs can create the carpet to complete the picture. *Leucojum vernum* (the spring snowflake) is a white and green tapestry beneath the early white blossom of *Prunus spinosa* var. *purpurea*, highlighted by a background of the dark green foliage and deep red flowers of *Rhododendron cornubia*. This is a striking red and white picture which brightens the dark days of late winter. The breathtaking white and violet picture of *Rhododendron* 'Florence Mann' beneath *Prunus* 'Mt Fuji' is completed in a most satisfying way with a carpet of white wood anemones (*Anemone nemorosa* var. *alba* or *A.n.* var. *bracteata*).

Alternatively, if a picture is satisfactory with just the tree and the shrubs, bulbs which flower at another time can be massed beneath them. The bulbs can be the stars themselves in their season, causing this section of the garden to feature twice during the year. Autumn-flowering crocuses such as *Crocus speciosus* provide a sheet of blue in autumn, just as they start into growth, and can be massed under open-growing trees which will feature in spring. *Chionodoxa sardensis* (the glory of the snow) creates a startling blue and white picture in late winter and can be massed in the foreground of trees and shrubs which will flower later.

From time to time throughout the text I have said in reference to specific bulbs that they must be kept dry in summer. Gardeners in areas of summer rainfall and summer humidity may think that their climate

The Spanish bluebell,
Hyacinthoides hispanica, is
larger and sturdier than the
English one, and even more
drought- and heat-tolerant.

Crocus tommasinianus with *Erica darleyensis* in a rock-garden which, although sunny for much of the day, is mulched by nearby trees.

precludes them from growing bulbs. This is not so. Bulbous plants which are dormant in summer will present the most difficulty because warm moist soil will cause many to rot. But, in the dappled shade of an urban woodland, the soil stays relatively cool, and ground-cover plants can be used above the bulbs to absorb excess moisture.

Summer-growing bulbs and perennials, both native and exotic, will of course be even more suitable, revelling in such conditions. Within the following genera some or all species are summer-growing: *Gladiolus*, *Hymenocallis*, *Hippeastrum*, *Habranthus*, *Zephyranthes*, *Cyrtanthus*, *Lilium* and many of the hardy orchids. In gardens which experience dry summers, these plants must be given an area which can be watered in summer, which drains well in winter and which has protection from frost. Alternatively, double-layer planting is an interesting idea, whereby winter-growing bulbs are planted above or among the summer-growers, providing frost protection and absorbing excess moisture in winter. This latter function is reversed in the summer. The area will still require summer watering, but it does have the advantage of providing the lower level of the picture twice in the year.

Gardeners in the north-east of Australia in subtropical climates experiencing monsoonal rains will find that the growing of summer-dormant bulbs is not worthwhile. As there are few deciduous trees and shrubs suitable for such areas, it is unlikely to be a deciduous woodland where winter sun penetrates, and the humidity in summer is too high to allow for successful dormancy. But, summer-growing bulbous plants

Helleborus orientalis is a versatile perennial for cool or warm temperate conditions, tolerating any degree of shade in summer, and naturalizing in woodland conditions.

A charming and elegant woodland perennial, *Dicentra formosa*, is very effective beneath late-flowering blossom trees.

will be a joy from September until April, and will be easier to grow in this climate than in areas with dry summers.

Selecting bulbs and perennials

As you begin to seek out the bulbs and perennials for your urban woodland, you will find that although a large range of woodland plants is available in Australia, many are to date only sold by specialist nurseries. The choice of these plants in general nurseries is usually limited. These nurseries stock according to demand. I am sure that as more people require a greater variety of woodland plants, the supply will adjust to meet this demand. Growers always watch for changing trends in plant requirements and produce accordingly.

Do not be discouraged if all the plants you desire are not available at the first nursery you visit. Be prepared to shop around a little for those special plants, just as you would for a particular item for the household. In the process you will come to know which nurseries are best for each type of plant, and you may find a plant which you thought was not available at all, or someone who has access to exactly what you require.

For those with a rock garden or sunny corner this non-invasive oxalis (*Oxalis hirta* var. *rosea*) is a joy in autumn and winter. Plant it above a bulb which will grow and flower in summer while the oxalis is dormant.

ON GROUND COVER

On any bare soil a plant will grow.
Better that it be one to suit your need
Than a greedy garden-robber
Or a rank and untidy weed.

The term 'ground cover' is generally applied to evergreen, low-growing plants which cover the ground with their leaves, thus keeping the soil cool and smothering many weeds. The weeds receive neither enough light nor enough nourishment to enable them to survive.

Ground-cover plants fall into several categories according to their habit of growth. There are those which cover large areas quickly by making new roots at every leaf-node. Others spread underground and make new shoots from every root. Some low shrubs form thickets by suckering. Many low-growing plants radiate out from a central root-stock. There are also many dense, low-growing shrubs and subshrubs. A large number of evergreen perennials make large clumps. Some of the herbaceous perennials and bulbous plants are also suitable for ground cover.

Type of ground cover
The most commonly used plants are those which cover large areas quickly by making a new shoot at every leaf-node. Hence they are the most readily available, if not from a nursery then from another gardener. Anyone who has any of these plants established will have plenty to spare. Because they make new roots so often, the denser-growing plants in this group will quickly cover the ground and smother the weeds. Unfortunately many such plants also smother anything else near them; they revel in most climatic conditions and become rampant. Although they are therefore useful in some areas of a garden, they must be used with discrimination.

Some, such as the aluminium plant (now called. *Lamiastrum galeobdolon*) and the variegated form of dwarf catmint (*Nepeta* 'Topsy') are very effective foliage plants for brightening a dark spot. The alpine strawberry (*Fragaria vesca*) very quickly covers the ground in semi-shade or even full shade, and provides interest throughout the year with its leaves, flowers or fruits. Although these three would be classed as rampant, they are shallow-rooted and thus quite easy to keep within bounds.

There are also some plants in this group which spread quite rapidly and make effective ground cover, but they do so in a more genteel manner. The various forms of ajuga are examples and mother-of-thousands (*Saxifraga stolonifera*) is usually quite well-behaved. The very flat carpeters such as Corsican mint, pratias and raoulias are also easily controlled, although not quite so good at smothering weeds.

Ground-cover plants which spread underground, sending up new shoots from every root, are the most rampant of all. In a sunny position, snow-in-summer (*Cerastium tomentosum*) makes a dense cover of silver foliage with white flowers above. It is a beautiful plant, but it insidiously takes over and is then very difficult to eradicate from areas where it is not wanted. Another plant which is showing signs of taking over large areas in my garden is *Nierembergia rivularis*. It is making very dense 5 cm high cover with its shiny green, lance-shaped leaves. It is a valuable ground plant, for in summer it is covered with large, white, saucer-shaped flowers. In my garden it is beginning to mingle with a border of *Gentiana septemfida* which flows over a rock edge. I think this will be a successful blue and white summer picture.

Many low shrubs create ground cover by suckering, forming dense thickets. Probably the best known and most rampant of these is rose of Sharon (*Hypericum calycinum*). It makes a dense, luxuriant ground cover, 30 cm high and flowers all through summer and autumn. But, I cannot recommend it to anyone with a small garden, for it is virtually impossible to eradicate later. As more and more good ground covers are becoming available, you do not have to resort to those which are virtually weeds. Some of the other hypericums, although not such good ground covers, are more garden worthy.

A large number of plants send out ground-hugging shoots in all directions from a central root system. These shoots, or branches, rarely make roots unless they are layered. This group make well-behaved ground-cover plants and, although you will need to buy more of them to cover a given area, they at least stay where you put them. The majority are sun-lovers and tend to become straggly in shade. Some I recommend for areas which receive a fair amount of sun each day. This category includes *Lithospermum* 'Grace Ward' which tends to be untidy in winter but provides a sea of deep blue flowers in spring, and the rock phloxes, *Phlox douglasii* and *P. subulata*, which are both available in several colours and will sometimes root as they spread.

Many of this group and also many of the dwarf shrubs cannot be grown in shade, even lightly dappled, under trees. This is not because they dislike shade, in fact they can be grown where they are in solid shade cast by a building or fence for part of the day, but because they are alpines or subalpines. In their natural habitat they may be shaded for part of the day by rocks, but they have evolved in such a way that they require intense light and crisp, fresh air. They will not tolerate drips from trees or damp leaves falling upon them. Many make excellent ground cover in a rock-garden, or even the open, sunny edge of a garden bed, but they do not succeed as woodlanders.

My favourite plants

My favourite ground-cover plants are perennials, some of them not quite evergreen, but growing long enough to deter weeds. The Lenten rose (*Helleborus orientalis*) makes bold ground cover with large, dark green leaves. The leaves will sometimes look a little ragged by early winter, but will be quickly replaced by new leaves during the flowering season. The hellebore flowers for five to six months in winter and spring, producing clusters of large, saucer-shaped flowers which bow

their heads shyly. The long-lasting blooms come in unusual shades of greenish-white, dusty pink and purplish-maroon. When this hellebore settles in and begins to seed itself about, you will have the full range of these colours, and any which may be dirty pinks or muddy purples are easily removed. It is said to require damp, shady positions, but in my garden it survived the recent drought and even bounced back after being burnt on Ash Wednesday.

The lady's mantle (*Alchemilla mollis*) is at last becoming available. I think it has the most beautiful foliage of any plant. The roundly-palmate leaves are pleated like a fan. They are soft green but at times take on a silver sheen. The surface is downy, and these little hairs trap raindrops which sparkle on the leaves. This is a low ground-cover plant in winter and spring, but then in summer the large, branched flower heads rise 50 cm above the foliage. These are massed with small, yellowish-green stars, which look so cool and fresh in the summer heat. In some gardens this lovely plant seeds itself too readily, but the young seedlings are easily removed, and will be gratefully accepted by any gardener without at least one patch of the plant.

I have a corydalis which is a treasure. It seeds itself readily so I am sure it will begin to appear in nurseries soon. In an old gardening book it is referred to as *Corydalis ochroleuca*, but I think it may be the pale

Helleborus orientalis provides winter pleasure and the strains available here are quite hardy.

Epimedium youngianum var. *niveum* will quickly make drifts of attractive ground cover.

form of *C. lutea*, which was once common in English gardens. The whole plant has a look of delicacy. The soft, greyish-green leaves are fern-like and the flowers are cream, tipped with gold. It seems never to stop flowering, and it does not die down. I suspect that each plant may be short-lived, but a colony is rapidly formed so that there will always be a good cover of fresh young plants.

Epimediums are proving to be good ground cover in my garden. They do have a short dormancy, but this is in winter when any self-respecting weed ought also to be dormant. *E. youngianum* var. *niveum* is a dwarf form which has lovely white 'Bishop's hat' flowers. The small, heart-shaped leaves are copper when new, becoming shining, bright green. *E. versicolour* var. *sulphureum* is larger with yellow flowers and lovely bronze new foliage. It seems to be a little slower in making good cover, but it is worth persevering with.

Selecting ground-cover plants

When choosing ground-cover plants, consider not only their ability to reduce maintenance, but also consider them for what they offer individually, or for their contribution to a picture. If used for foliage effects of colour, shape or texture, or even simply as a contrast to the leaves of plants nearby, they can add a great deal of interest to your

garden. Many of course have beautiful flowers and can create the carpet of a planned picture. Some take on beautiful tints of bronze, pink or red in the winter, and seem to emerge after the trees and shrubs above have lost their leaves. A few can be used as a carpet for woodland bulbs, but they must be strong enough to hold their own when tree roots are active, and yet not so vigorous as to deprive the bulbs of nourishment when they require it.

This chapter has merely scratched the surface of what is a large and important area of gardening, and I strongly recommend that you read one of the books that discuss ground cover in depth. Your biggest decision regarding ground plants in general will be whether to cover the ground quickly and effectively with those that will become rampant, or whether to keep these out of your garden altogether and take more time achieving good cover with choicer plants. In the long-term those which are fast movers will smother any which are more tardy. It becomes a great deal of work to keep them separated, particularly in a small suburban garden. This then defeats one of the purposes of using ground cover, that of reducing garden maintenance. It is just as difficult to remove unwanted ground-cover plants as it is to remove weeds.

Violets are traditionally ground-cover plants for shady positions. More species are becoming available, providing an interesting range of leaf shade, shape and texture as well as flower colour.

ON ESTABLISHMENT

Observe the ways of nature in your garden.
Watch the cycles of the chosen plants and weeds.
For by understanding all their different habits
You will learn to control them to suit your needs.

This is a difficult time for a gardener. The excitement of planning and the satisfaction of planting are over. Now your attention is turned towards searching for signs of any setback in the plants. The weather seems to be always too hot or too cold, or too dry or too wet. The winds seem to be stronger than in other years. Worrying afterthoughts keep niggling you regarding the depth of planting, the teasing of roots and other vital issues.

To retain your sanity while your new garden is establishing, you need confidence and work. Have confidence in yourself and the way you have done the job (or in the person who constructed the garden for you). Have confidence in your nursery staff and the quality of the plants provided. Perhaps most importantly have confidence in nature which provided plants with the resilience to recover from the trauma of being transplanted. Occupy yourself with the work required to enable your garden to establish itself. For a new garden to survive its first summer it needs to be mulched, weeded and watered. (Gardeners with the luxury of summer rainfall may neglect the latter chore and turn all their attention to the weeds.)

Mulching

The importance of mulch is discussed in detail in another chapter. I would like to stress here that a new garden is not finished until it is thoroughly mulched. In some areas which have never been mulched, and particularly on light soils, the first cover of mulch will seem to disappear. If this is the case, it is worthwhile applying another layer. In fact, any time that bare soil is observed, more mulch should be applied. As your garden becomes established this will happen less often.

Weeding

No matter how thoroughly you remove the roots of perennial weeds before planting, some will reappear in the newly-planted garden. In the first growing season after planting, you should consistently remove weeds as they appear. Do not leave them to compete with the establishing roots of the young plants. If your garden is large, or if you do not have much time to spend in it, I would suggest that you plant and establish your urban woodland in stages. The level of maintenance is high during the first year of a new garden, no matter what its style.

There would be less maintenance in this vital first year if the weeds were killed first. But, I cannot recommend that you resort to using chemicals. In 15 years of gardening I have never sprayed a weedicide,

herbicide, fungicide or insecticide in my garden. (I did once put down snail bait, but when the dog ate some and became sick I gave that away too.) I am conscious of the useful bacteria and other micro-organisms which keep the soil healthy, and of the worms which work so hard at the same job, and I wonder how chemicals would affect them. I also wonder what long-term effect, perhaps as yet unforeseen, chemical residues may have on garden soils.

Despite these personal doubts about the use of garden chemicals in general, there are some hormonal weed killers available which are reputed to break down on contact with water and to leave no residue in the soil. I do not know whether their effect on micro-organisms and worms has been studied. Until I am convinced that these are not adversely affected, I will continue to keep myself and the soil healthy by removing the weeds myself.

I used to regard weeding as the necessary evil associated with the otherwise enchanting hobby of gardening. I would put it off, often until the seed had dispersed ensuring a good crop of weeds for the following year. I would grumble, as many people do, about the beds which needed weeding. Slowly my attitude changed, in the following manner:

> When our children were small, and my daytime hours in the garden were limited, I fell into the habit of escaping outside for the last hour of light in the summer; that lovely hour, when the children are in bed and the chores are done (or perhaps they're not, but they can be done after dark). The

Eighteen months after planting, this rock garden is established and virtually maintenance-free.

garden takes on a new fresh look and has a shimmering iridescence in the evening light. As I was determined not to become a habitual waterer, I found that instead of sprinkling with a hose I was pulling weeds as I wandered about; at first haphazardly here and there, and then systematically working through the beds.

When you unconsciously weed in this manner, although ever alert to the chance discovery of a seedling of a precious gem, your mind wanders into dreams. After spending an hour or so in this way, when gathering dusk awoke me from my reverie, I was always surprised to notice how much weeding I had done without thinking about it.

The children are no longer small, but I still enjoy that evening hour of solitude, or of companionship if one of the family is with me. My attitude to it is somewhat different; I have a comfortable kneeler, and I call it my 'weeding hour', so perhaps some of the charm is lost. However I have never made such a ritual of it that I feel compelled to weed at this time. I don't force myself to do it if I am tired or otherwise indisposed, for I would once again be grumbling about the weeding. Sometimes my husband and I use this hour just to wander in the garden, discussing plans for it, and pulling weeds haphazardly as in the early years.

However this hour is spent, I still feel annoyed when daylight saving ends for I know that in a week or two my gardening activities will be restricted to the daytime. But at whatever time of day I find myself weeding, my mind is relaxed and I no longer consider it an onerous task.

There is one point well worth remembering regarding weeds and their growth; they will set their seed and disperse it far more quickly if they are parched and struggling. If weeds, or any plants for that matter, are growing lushly and are healthy, they grow and flourish for their full season before setting seed. If they are starved and in threat of death, they will quickly run up to seed to perpetuate the species. Thus it is not wise to leave a weedy patch of ground which is not receiving water and in which the weeds are drooping, thinking that those weeds will probably die anyway, and to turn your energies to the beds where weeds are flourishing. Yes, those neglected weeds probably will die, but not before they have seeded around your garden. This would be long before the healthy weeds which you have carefully extracted would have completed their cycle.

Watering

Along with mulching and weeding, watering is an essential ingredient of successful establishment of a garden. The principles and practices of watering are discussed fully in another chapter. It is a necessary chore during this first summer, but please don't become carried away with it. I know that watering the garden is a pleasant and traditional way to spend the evening of a hot day. If you find that you have the tendency to fall into this habit, you must be firm with yourself. Use a sprinkler when the garden needs water, adjust it to cover only the area which requires it, and then leave it alone for at least an hour. You cannot give a deep enough soaking by standing with a hand-held hose, so the temptation is to wander around and give everything a little drink. The gardener who applies weekly soakings to a new garden rather than nightly sprinklings uses far less water, and has a garden full of deep-rooted, drought-resistant plants. Ten-day intervals between soakings is

Gardens can quickly become 'over-established'. I love the wild charm of this corner, but it would still be nice with a little thinning out. It is a matter of taste as to the degree of establishment required.

In a fully-established and easily-maintained garden, even the path will not get weedy if the weeds in the garden beds are removed before they can sow their seeds into it.

generally sufficient in the second year, and thereafter fortnightly or no watering at all, depending upon the type of plants which you have established.

After establishment

It always amazes me how quickly this irksome stage of establishment is past. In the first year I struggle with a new bed, and wonder why I did such a large area at once. In the second year it takes me about an hour once a month to thoroughly weed this same bed. From the third year onwards it joins the rest of the garden in a spring and autumn clean-up. This is achieved partly because weeds are not allowed to seed, partly because the mulch is repressing many would-be-weeds, but mainly because an urban woodland planting is becoming established. The trees, shrubs and ground plants are spreading and shade is cast over the soil. It is a fact worth remembering that virtually all of the weeds are sun-lovers. They do not thrive in shade and, in fact, become steadily weaker until they cannot compete with the plants which revel in such conditions.

Front fences can be softened by an overflow of plants without intruding onto the footpath, giving the home a well-established look and adding to the pleasure of the passer-by.

ON LOW-MAINTENANCE GARDENING

When the cares of the workplace are behind you,
The gentle exercise of tending a garden
Promotes a healthy mind and body,
And gives purpose to the retirement years of your
life.

No garden can ever be completely maintenance-free, but certain types of gardens have lower levels of maintenance than others. You can have a desert of pebbles or tanbark on black plastic with hardy shrubs planted through holes in the plastic. But, for those who don't find this appealing, the urban woodland requires the least maintenance of all the pretty garden styles.

Why a lawn?
Before you plant a lawn, decide whether you really need it. Once planted, it will be the largest maintenance job of all. If your outdoor living area is paved, slated or cobbled, or is on a terrace or timber deck, you need have only a small area of shaded lawn for the hottest days. This need not even be of grass. There are many mat-forming plants which could be used, and for an area which is mainly sunny a thyme lawn is lovely.

If your children have a handy recreation area in the form of a park or playground, they need only a small area of native grass on which to roll and run. Most people do not have the space within their boundaries for ball-throwing, football or cricket, and you may find that children appreciate the paths and secret places of your garden more than an open backyard.

Not many people have the scope for a large sweep of lawn, which is most effective. If you cannot achieve this look, why plant a lawn in the front of your house and set yourself the task of the continual maintenance of it. The front lawn only looks good when regularly mowed, clipped, watered, weeded and fed, and surely a more pleasant approach to a house is along a path winding through carefully chosen trees, shrubs and ground plants. The maintenance thus required is not monotonous and continual. It becomes less and less as the plants grow and thicken until it reaches the stage where all that is necessary is an annual clean-up.

Necessary maintenance
The extent of maintenance depends on how tidy you wish your garden to be. There will be the occasional weed of course. If you like your garden to have a slightly wild look, no pruning is ever needed. If you want a very low-maintenance garden, you should not include any plant which *must* be regularly clipped, sprayed or fed. Many plants can be

induced to flower better or to have a better shape by judicious pruning, but will survive, look natural and flower sufficiently, without it.

Where possible purchase a species rather than a hybrid or cultivar. With continual breeding to produce larger flowers of different colours, many of the newer varieties seem to be more reliant upon extra feed and moisture than the parent which grew in the wild state without extra supplies of either. The rose is a good example. The roses which grew in the old cottage gardens are in many cases still growing there, never having been pruned or sprayed.

You will probably wish to rake leaves from the paths onto the garden, and you may wish to have a more formal area at the entrance which will require a little more work. Except in this formal setting, clipping of plants is unnecessary as the overflow of ground plants onto the paths gives the soft, natural look which is appropriate. If the original plan is sound, there will be no encroachment by trees and shrubs onto the paths.

There is no room for weeds in a garden such as this, where every bit of space is utilized leaving no bare soil for weed seeds to lodge in.

A further labour-saving feature of the urban woodland is that it is planted with deciduous trees (small-growing ones for small gardens, with some medium to tall-growing ones as well for large gardens) in preference to evergreens. The latter, particularly eucalypts, drop their litter of leaves, bark and twigs all year round, and in greater amounts in the summer months. If you like even a reasonably tidy garden, you are continually cleaning up this litter for which you then have no use unless you can stock-pile it for at least one year. The deciduous trees are much tidier. They hold their leaves until they have coloured then they drop them all at once, within a matter of weeks. Thus you have one cleaning-up time which only involves raking leaves onto the garden from the open areas.

No matter how well you mulch your garden or how thoughtfully you plan it, there will always be some weeds which persistently appear. You will lessen the problem if you pull them before they seed. The same applies to woodland annuals and biennials, such as forget-me-nots and foxgloves, which have the tendency to seed in places where you would rather they didn't. Allow them to flower for you in the picture you have planned, then pull them out before the seed escapes. If you plan a wild garden, let them seed and be surprised each year where they will pop up. If they spoil a special effect, they are easily removed.

Feeding of plants is another chore which could be unnecessary. You may wish to feed lightly in the early stages to encourage speedier growth, but really the mulching is sufficient. Remember that this is the only source of plant food provided naturally, other than nutrients existing in the soil. If you wish to incorporate into your garden a plant from an area of very rich soil, one which you know to be a gross feeder, then by all means give the plant its requirements but don't feel that you should feed everything else as well.

If you have been advised that your soil is lacking in certain ingredients essential to healthy growth, then it is of course worthwhile incorporating these. But do it cautiously, using just enough to restore the balance, as too much of any element will not be tolerated by many plants.

Using compost

In a garden situation, particularly that of the urban woodland style, trees and shrubs may be closer together than they would be in their natural state, or there may be more woodland plants competing for space beneath the trees. For this reason I like to use an annual layer of compost as well as the leaf mould. In addition to feeding, compost builds up the humus level, creating healthier soil.

As your compost will take about three months to reach a sweet and friable state, you could divide (in your mind) your garden roughly into four and apply a layer of compost as soon as it is ready to each section in turn, thus achieving an annual layer. The compost works its way slowly into the soil, feeding the roots as it goes, so it will be available to the plants at some stage during the following growing season. Even if you can make only enough compost to add to each section of the garden every second or third year, this is well worthwhile doing.

If this sounds like another tedious chore, think of it as only four half days of work in a year. As far as making the compost is concerned, a lot has been written and much research has been done, and you may wish to experiment yourself. Probably the enclosed-type of commercial compost bins are the most convenient for the suburban gardener.

Anything that has lived can become compost, and it is quite easy to place vegetable peelings and other similar kitchen refuse in the compost bin, and to chop and add garden refuse and papers. Do not add too much paper, sawdust or lawn clippings without mixing these with something which will not pack down, such as leaves.

I do not dig the compost into the soil. In fact I recommend that gardens are not dug at all after the initial hoeing prior to planting. It is another traditional gardening chore which is unnecessary and can be detrimental. Compost is best left as a top-dressing in the way the soil is annually top dressed with leaves or dying grasses and other material—returning to the soil what has been taken out by the roots. Worms will then take all this organic matter into the soil, creating better drainage and aerating the soil as they do so. Digging slows down the increase of worm populations. Recent studies in Britain and America have shown that worm casts are five times richer in nitrogen, seven times richer in phosphates and eleven times richer in potash than ordinary soil.

Hoeing and watering

Shallow hoeing has traditionally been a method of weeding. Admittedly it reduces the population of weed seedlings, but it is also the scarifying process for weed seeds, and thus encourages their development. A further reason for not digging over the garden, apart from the obvious one of disturbing the roots of your plants, is that 80 per cent or more of the necessary bacteria are in the top 8 to 10 centimetres of soil. If dug over to a spade's depth, which is traditional, these bacteria take some time to re-establish themselves near the surface. So do not dig unless necessary and, if you do, remember the roots, and the worms and the micro-organisms which keep your plants and your soil healthy.

A final word on garden maintenance concerns watering. If you plant shade trees (not necessarily large ones) and if you mulch liberally (the trees will do this for you when large enough), once your plants are established you need rarely, if ever, water your garden. Even for desert fringes there are some suitable deciduous trees which give protection as well as mulch. If you desire any plants from areas which have a much higher rainfall than your own, you will have to give them some water, especially while they are young.

Once the urban woodland is established, most of it will withstand drought conditions for a fortnight without suffering, some sections ten days, some sections one week, and other parts will cope until the inevitable rain arrives. It all depends on the type of plants and soil and the amount of shade and mulch.

Where a mixture of native and
exotic shrubs is grown, the
exotics add substance to the
design, and help to fill in this
area so that the ground is well
covered.

ON WATERING

*It is far better to grow plants which will adapt
to your conditions than to adapt your
conditions to suit the plants.*

Water is one of the most valuable resources, and with the world's
population increasing as it is, the time has come for people to learn to
conserve this resource as they are learning to conserve others. Millions
of litres of water could be saved annually if it was not poured
unnecessarily onto gardens, especially onto front lawns in order to
keep them green. Readers in summer rainfall areas may ignore the
following remarks, for they apply to those who feel the need to supple-
ment meagre summer rainfall by artificial watering.

Lawn and annuals
The watering habit in this country has its origins in the early settlers'
attempts to create an English environment around their homes. Lawn
seed brought out from England was sown and it germinated, but the
settlers soon discovered that the only way to keep it green throughout
the summer was to apply large quantities of water. The same applied to
the traditional summer-bedding plants. These flourished and flowered
well but wilted daily unless watered. As water storages were constructed
and piped water became available, so began the habit of nightly
sprinkling which has continued to this day. It is still the lawn and
annuals which benefit from this activity; nothing else in the garden
does, with the exception of vegetables. In this case the water is being
used to provide food.

This type of watering is detrimental to trees, shrubs, bulbs, ground
covers and most perennials. Are the lawns and beds of annuals really
necessary? Could that splendid summer display be achieved by using
another type of plant? The answer to this is yes. There are summer-
flowering forms of all the groups of plants mentioned, and many of
them, particularly bulbs, will actually flower better if water is withheld.
(It is also far less work to achieve your summer effect without annuals!)

Do we need all that lawn? The water that pours down countless
gutters daily from late spring until mid-autumn could be saved if we
could bring ourselves to dig up that lawn and replace it with a well-
planned, low-maintenance garden. Even in its early years this type of
garden will require much less water than a well-maintained lawn.

Using deciduous trees
If you are in the south-east of Australia, it is possible that your garden
as a whole may be more resistant to summer drought if the trees in it
are deciduous exotics rather than the types of native trees which are
generally available in nurseries. I say this because the native trees are

usually from drier areas, and have evolved in such a way that they absorb every drop of moisture when it is available, leaving the soil as dry as dust again. In a garden situation this causes all other plants in the vicinity, including lawn, to suffer.

Many of the deciduous trees which are readily available come from those areas of Europe, North America and Asia where the climate is similar to that of south-eastern Australia. They appreciate spring rain, but don't expect much in summer. They mulch their own root system which protects the surface-feeding roots from frost in winter, feeds the tree as the leaves decompose and lasts long enough to keep the root system cool and moist during the summer.

As spring rains cease and the weather becomes hotter, deciduous trees slow down their growth while their new wood ripens and hardens so as to be less susceptible to frost. They conserve moisture at this stage and appear to settle down to wait until they can show off in a blaze of autumn colour, then drop their leaves to replenish their mulch. Other plants in the vicinity of these trees are bound to benefit.

Corners, such as this, shaded by deciduous trees remain cool and moist enough even for plants such as fuchsias to survive without watering.

On a hot day in summer, if you feel the soil under the mulch of a deciduous tree and the soil under a dry-area native (even if it is mulched), you will notice the difference. If more natives of south-eastern Australia were available, they would be more suitable there. Tasmania has some wonderful trees and shrubs which would be good for Melbourne gardens if evergreens are required.

Effects of unnecessary watering
Thus water is more important to your garden in spring than it is in summer. As well as those deciduous trees mentioned, most other non-tropical plants grow vigorously while spring rains last, and slow down their growth as summer progresses. They can even stop growing completely during a prolonged dry spell to conserve their available moisture, then sprout again after rain. Unnecessary watering during dry weather forces tender new growth which has to contend with the extreme heat of the sun, and either burns or droops, thus requiring more water. It can become a vicious circle, broken only by the gardener's strength of will.

It is a sad fact that the burnt or drooping plants often seen in summer are suffering not from under-watering, but from over-watering. Left alone, the plant would have known better than to produce that last bit of new growth until there had been rain, and cooler weather arrived. This is their natural way of coping with drought.

Drip and trickle systems
Much is being written at present about drip and trickle irrigation systems. They are being promoted as the answer to water problems, but I have certain reservations about their value to the home gardener.

I concede that these systems do cut down on the loss of water due to evaporation and run-off and, if installed and used correctly, can keep the level of moisture in the soil constant. I think that they are suitable for many farmers, particularly market gardeners, for in their case the vegetables and flowers are being replanted each year, providing an annual opportunity for maintenance of the system. For this reason they are also suitable for the home vegetable garden or for any area which is renewed each year. This type of watering would also be good for rock gardens where alpines are grown, for in the wild much of their water is provided by gradually-melting snow. Many of them prefer not to be watered overhead.

But I am not convinced that keeping the soil constantly moist is good for the garden as a whole. For a plant to complete a natural life cycle it must have a natural annual cycle each year. If that cycle includes the slowing down of growth in the heat of the summer to allow for the ripening of new wood, then surely this should happen. Many plants also initiate flower buds at this time and will not flower well during the following season if kept growing right through the summer.

Gardeners should attempt to imitate, not change, nature. As a bulbgrower I shudder when I see a spring-flowering bulb in bloom in winter, for I know that the bulb has been forced, which has severely weakened it, perhaps unto death. When I see a tree which has put on three years growth in one season I wonder whether it has thus lost two years off its life or if the damage is even more severe.

For gardeners prepared to use drip-watering to give plants a thorough, deep soaking occasionally, the system still presents some problems. If the pipes are laid on the surface of the garden they will deteriorate rapidly in the heat and in the cold. The water in these pipes will be extremely hot in the summer, at times hot enough to severely damage the roots of plants. Gardeners will be less inclined to mulch thoroughly each year, for this will mean either lifting all the pipes, or burying them under the mulch. Mulch is a greater water saver than any watering system can be.

If the pipes are buried initially or by mulching, the outlets will soon become clogged, if not by soil then by water-seeking roots, very quickly rendering the system ineffective. Maintenance will be more difficult and may cause damage to the roots of plants. As your garden becomes established, whether the pipes are on the surface or not, plants may be damaged as you perform the annual servicing which is necessary to maintain this type of system in good working order.

Perhaps the greatest long-term problem with drip-watering, as with any automatic system, is the tendency for over-use. The temptation with these systems is to activate them whenever the weather becomes hot or the surface of the soil or mulch looks dry. If you have to go out and set up a sprinkler or stand and hold a hose, you are more likely to stop and wonder whether the garden really does need water. If it does, then the overhead watering, as well as replacing soil moisture, imitates rain and washes the pollution off the leaves, freshening them and allowing them to breathe again.

If automatic watering appeals to you, then it is very cheap to set it up, with each new section of garden containing a section of soaker hose attached to a timer. When the soaker deteriorates beyond use, in about three or more years, it need not be replaced as that section of garden will then be established. From then on it may not grow as rapidly each year as a constantly moist garden, but the plants will be hardy, healthy and bursting with flowers.

Hardy plants

The term 'hardy' with regard to plants has come to mean the ability to stand the cold of winter in the open ground, because this is the worst extreme which a plant has to tolerate in the English climate. For Australian conditions, I use the word 'hardy' to describe a plant which will stand heat and drought as well as cold. Thus a plant which is hardy in your garden can tolerate the worst extremes to which the climate will submit it. Obviously not all plants will be hardy in any one area, but the way in which plants are treated certainly has a bearing on their ability to survive extremes.

Plants from those areas of the northern hemisphere which have a cooler, moister climate than most of Australia, will adapt to conditions in many areas and become hardy if treated with the weaning procedure described below in conjunction with liberal mulching and protection from hot, drying winds. You may find that weekly watering will be

Permanent water in your garden, provided that there is a certain amount of seepage at the edges, can create areas of damp soil which provide homes for plants otherwise requiring copious amounts of artificial watering.

necessary for several years if the wind barrier is not established, or, in the case of woodland plants, until the trees are providing shade. It is interesting to note that the bulbs and herbaceous plants which require a cool moist growing season are dormant during the heat of the summer, and that those still growing and flowering in summer enjoy the heat and require no more water than the rest of the garden.

Weaning process

Any new plant purchased will need to be gradually weaned from the copious amounts of water it has received in the nursery. In the nursery situation, plants in pots must be watered daily in summer to be kept in peak condition. Once planted in your garden, watered-in thoroughly and mulched well, each plant may need to be water again two or three days later, depending on the moisture-holding capacity of your soil. The time between watering is then gradually increased until you are giving weekly soakings to each plant in its first summer. This process encourages the roots to go in search of moisture and promotes a stronger, deeper root system.

During the following spring and autumn, ten-day intervals will be enough for most plants. From the third year onwards, watering will only be necessary during prolonged dry spells, or not at all, for the plant is well-established with a deep root system. Plants with shallow root systems may need watering more often, although I have found that even rhododendrons and azaleas, once established, are extremely hardy, for they shelter their own root systems keeping them cool and moist. Rock-garden plants will send their roots under the rocks to keep them cool.

In the case of an established garden, which has always been watered regularly, the weaning process will also be necessary. Even the oldest trees may not have developed deep water-searching roots if water has always been available near the surface. You should spend the first year making sure that each soaking wets the soil below the existing root system and wait as long as possible before repeating the procedure. By the following summer your garden should be ready for you to join the non-waterers.

Correct watering

If you are in an area which has water restrictions in summer, and if you feel that your garden must be watered, then do it correctly. Use a two-hour watering session to water only one section of your garden. Soak it thoroughly, then forget that area for at least ten days. In your next watering session, do another section thoroughly, and continue this procedure until you are back to the first area again. Don't feel that in your watering time you must give everything a drink. This would only serve to keep the roots of all your plants close to the surface, and make your garden more drought-prone.

All this points to the fact that within two to five years, depending on the plants chosen, your garden will have reached the stage where it only requires artificial watering in drought times, and even then will

probably survive if water is not available. During these early years you will learn which plants in your garden show signs of needing more water than others. With these you must be firm enough to soak them thoroughly and wait as long as possible before the next soaking, as some plants require more encouragement to establish a deep root system than others. You will also learn to notice the various symptoms of thirst in your garden and to respond to these before plants are wilting badly. Wilting is a sign of severe stress from which some plants may not recover.

The procedure for non-watering is this; only water a plant when it is visibly showing the desire for it, and then give *only that plant* a thorough soaking. You will end up with not only less work, but a garden full of hardier plants. Remember that once you make your garden depend on the artificial aid of regular watering, you have condemned yourself to join the garden waterers for the rest of the summer.

ON MULCH

Despair not when leaves begin to fall,
For the returning to the soil of the goodness
removed
Is part of the natural cycle of a healthy garden.

You may read a great deal about mulching gardens, but do you really understand why? There are many ways in which mulch saves work and improves your garden at the same time. I like to compare my layer of mulch to the insulation in the ceiling, for it insulates the soil in a similar way. In summer it keeps the heat out so that the roots don't burn, and in winter it retains the warmth that is in the soil for the root systems.

Advantages of mulch
Mulch cuts down on watering because it absorbs and holds the water, so that the soil does not dry out as quickly as it otherwise would. It cuts down on weeding because it smothers most weeds as they germinate and stops others from germinating. It cuts down on feeding because, provided you use mulch that is not completely decomposed, the breaking-down process feeds the plants. A layer of mulch on sloping ground helps to hold the soil in place until plants can achieve this, and lessens run off of water. Thus only very steep slopes need terracing.

Cyclamen hederifolium naturalizes in leaf mould. Each year the new layer of leaf litter protects the seed until germination and keeps the soil cool around the young seedlings.

Another advantage of mulch is the long-term effect it has on improving the soil quality and texture. On heavy soils, the leaf mould (as decomposing leaves are called) serves to open and enrich the soil. The soil becomes much more friable. On sandy soils the effect is added body. In either case, what you end up with is something akin to good mountain soil. Also, continual mulching with leaves gradually increases acidity in areas of alkaline soils. Many of the favoured garden plants prefer a slightly acid soil.

All garden plants appreciate mulching. This is because plants in their wild state are mulched naturally. Most of the earth's land masses were originally forests and even plants from the alpine areas 'above the forests' and from the desert fringes 'below the forests' are accustomed to mulch in the form of dying grasses and leaves which they shed themselves. Mat-forming alpines must only be mulched around their roots, and never on their leaves.

Have you ever wondered why such shrubs as azaleas, rhododendrons and camellias are so shallow-rooted, or why trees and shrubs in general have their feeding roots so close to the surface? It is because this is where the annual supply of plant food should be. When using liquid manures or fertilizers, you have to continually repeat the process; not necessarily because the plants have gobbled up what you gave them, but because it has washed down to a level below the feeding roots. The roots may follow it down, but then they are below the level of essential ingredients found in surface soil.

Bulbs that grow naturally under trees cannot survive without mulch. Take the woodland cyclamen as an example. Each year the corm is pushed up to grow in the mulch, and the seeds are ejected to germinate in the mulch. The cyclamen corm would shrivel and die without mulch, and how would the seeds germinate to increase the clump? Many crocus species produce their new bulb on top of the old, so the crocus clump would not multiply without the mulch.

Some think that mulching the whole garden is just another chore. Plan your garden so that it mulches itself and, until it can, buy or acquire some mulch each year (you might know of someone who actually burns leaves), for this is far less tedious than continually watering, weeding and feeding.

Types of mulch

Leaves from deciduous trees are the best mulch to use. The urban woodland of course supplies its own in areas where deciduous trees can be used. It will take from three to six years (depending on the number, type and size of deciduous trees and shrubs used) for the newly-planted garden to be self-sufficient in this regard. It is unlikely that you will ever get to the stage where you feel that you have far too many leaves for your garden's needs, because even a 15 centimetre layer of leaves will only become a 2 to 4 centimetre layer of leaf mould and this decomposes leaving the soil level barely raised. However, if there is any excess it is a good idea to stockpile the leaves to incorporate in your compost bin, or to be used during the summer months as mulch for the

Straw can be used as mulch if leaves are not available, and does look quite attractive once it mellows in colour.

vegetable garden, plants in pots, or as an extra feed for areas of the garden that are growing rapidly.

Grass clippings can be incorporated with the leaves but should not be used on their own. There are two reasons for this. They have a tendency to pack rather hard and to form a smooth skin on top. Water runs off this instead of soaking in. Under this skin an excessive amount of heat builds up, far more than plants desire during an Australian summer. So if grass clippings are the only mulching material available to you, remember to regularly break the skin with a fork to let the heat out and the water in.

In very frosty areas, where a winter mulch can be as important as a summer mulch, grass clippings are more useful, especially if applied in autumn, as they keep the soil warmer throughout winter. Autumn is the time when leaf mulch naturally occurs, but as winters are generally not as harsh as in the areas where deciduous trees are indigenous, it is not necessary in most parts of Australia to artificially mulch until October or November.

Be very wary of sawdust as mulch. Instead of feeding the plants, it robs them of precious nitrogen unless it is already completely decomposed and, at this stage, it does not feed them anyway. Tanbark is attractive and long-lasting as mulch, but decomposes too slowly to be a worthwhile source of plant food or to be a soil improver. Pine bark, which is usually sold in large pieces, is even less useful from this point of view and is too large for small woodland plants to struggle through. Eucalypt leaves are best stockpiled for a year or two before being used as a mulch, as they take a long time to break down and thin layers of them take even longer. Mushroom bed compost is good if old, but often when purchased the manure in it is so fresh that it burns plants, and it is often quite alkaline.

Although there appears to be nothing quite as good for mulch as autumn leaves, any of the other sources of mulching material is better than no mulch at all. You should aim to apply a layer 7 to 10 centimetres thick, and no more than 15 centimetres. The latter would apply only to freshly-fallen leaves in autumn, which would settle to become a much thinner layer — never apply artificial mulch as thickly as this. It is a good idea to apply your mulch when the ground is already wet. This moisture will then be retained by the mulch. After applying a mulch such as grass clippings, peat, straw or sawdust, wet it thoroughly using a fine spray so that it doesn't pack hard.

This Japanese maple, which is less than ten years old, is satisfactorily mulching quite a large area beneath and around itself.

IN CONCLUSION

If your garden is your life,
Your life in the garden will be a happy one,
Filled with the joy and contentment
That the creation of living beauty can give.

If your garden is your hobby,
It will be a satisfying and an absorbing one.
And as your garden grows it will grow on you
Until one day you may realize that
Your garden is your life.

Most of my gardening experience has been in cool temperate and cool mountainous regions. I apologize to readers with different conditions for the fact that most of the plants shown in the photographs and mentioned in the text are those suitable for these two climatic zones. I hope you will understand that I feel most competent to write about those plants with which I am familiar. However, as a result of research, observations when travelling, and discussions with gardeners in other areas, I hope I have been able to include enough information to enable a gardener anywhere in Australia to create an urban woodland.

It may be helpful for readers to know the conditions under which my plants are grown. Soil was virtually non-existent; one small area had a little topsoil, and the rest of the block was clay. I have not imported any soil, but the annual top-dressing of humus is gradually improving the quality and texture of the garden beds. The temperature ranges from −6°C to 40°C and on rare occasions is outside this range. The rainfall basically coincides with the coldest months, from June until December. The other six months are warm to hot and dry. There is invariably three weeks without rain, and quite often longer than this. Thus the climate is colder and wetter in winter and spring than that of Melbourne, and hotter and drier in summer and autumn. Many gardeners in Australia experience a climate similar to this, with cool or cold winters, warm to hot summers and reasonable rainfall in winter and (to a lesser extent) spring.

Gardeners in many parts of Sydney can have the best of both gardening worlds. Winters are cool and moist enough for temperate climate (and in some cases cool climate) plants to thrive, and summers are warm and moist enough for growing subtropical plants. Woodland gardens can be created where European, Asian and American deciduous trees are underplanted with bold-foliaged, tropical-looking plants, both native and exotic. The contrast is extremely effective in all seasons. The choice of possible planting combinations for an urban woodland in Sydney is endless, and is the envy of gardeners who are limited by the fact that their annual rainfall is predominantly in one season.

Wherever you live, it is important to use plants which you know to be suitable for the climate and soil-type of your area, particularly in the beginning. Gardening becomes an expensive hobby when plants die due to unsuitability. Many plants also die because they are purchased before the garden is ready to receive them. They sit in their pots, deprived of the regular watering, feeding and repotting to which they had become accustomed. They may often need replacing by the time the gardener is ready to plant them. It is a good idea to check on the availability of your chosen plants well in advance of planting time, and even to place orders for them, but never bring them home until you are completely ready to plant and mulch them.

The seven principles which I have discussed as necessary elements of the urban woodland design are not new ideas. Most have been advocated at some time in the history of gardening. Perhaps each new generation of garden designers has nothing more innovative to offer than personal interpretations of sound gardening principles, and the development of these to suit the time and place. To reiterate, these principles are:

1   Segment your garden so that it is not all seen at once. This will make your garden seem larger than it is, and at the same time will shorten the view so that each picture is seen and appreciated individually.

2   Cover the ground with plants so that no bare earth is seen. This not only cuts down on maintenance, but also gives your garden a well-furnished look right from the beginning.

3   Have as little lawn as possible, particularly if your block is small. This is even more important in areas with dry summers, for it is a temptation to try to keep the lawn green by applying copious amounts of water.

4   Soften all edges and corners, except where you desire a more formal setting. This gives the garden a natural and well-established appearance.

5   Design the garden to suit the house. The result is that your house either blends into the garden or is enhanced by it.

6   Do not think of the urban woodland as a static design. Over the years you may make many changes, because your knowledge of plants and their uses will increase, because your personal tastes will vary, and because conditions in your garden will alter. But, I hope that your changes will never be merely for the sake of fashion. When you do choose, for whatever reason, to add new plants, don't forget to include them in an appropriate picture or to create a picture which will display them to their best advantage.

7   Keep maintenance levels as low as possible so that you have time to relax in and enjoy this beautiful creation of yours.

If your urban woodland is designed with these seven principles in mind and if it is carefully picture-planned employing the methods and suggestions mentioned throughout the text, it will be a garden of intricate textures, with infinite variety of shades and shapes. It will be a harmonious garden—in harmony with the house, its owners, and the birds that will certainly inhabit it, and in which all the plants are in harmony with each other.

Your urban woodland may also prove to be an outlet for your artistic talent, for I am sure that there is a little of the artist in us all, even those of us not skilled with pen or brush. Your land is the canvas on which you create your living work of art. Unlike a two-dimensional art work, you can remove your mistakes, make changes at any time, and watch it grow into a complete, mature, living monument to your horticultural preferences, taste and artistic ability.

The urban woodland is for those who love their garden not just for its spring beauty, but who love dappled shade on cottage flowers or tropical treasures in summer, a blaze of glory in autumn, and winter sun shining through bare branches onto masses of woodland or rainforest gems.

In today's society, where environment protection has an ever-increasing importance, it is worth remembering that plants are nature's air filters and that the denser the planting the more efficient the filter. By creating an urban woodland you will be providing your home with an antipollution device as well as beautifying your neighbourhood.

A pleasant mixture of dry climate natives and exotics. The dense planting beneath the young eucalypt may be difficult to maintain in future years.

In each of these heavily-planted, low-maintenance gardens, the deciduous trees are close to the house, and the open areas near the boundaries allow for picture-planning with sun-loving plants.

THE PLANS

Within the following plans I have endeavoured to suggest only those plants which are available in Australia. Most are easily obtained, some are available only from specialist growers, and a few will require tracking down, for they are not always obtainable. Thus I have used some plants which are considered common and as such are scorned by some gardeners. But I have endeavoured to show that even the most common plant can become a wonderful feature of your garden when used in a suitable setting. Conversely, I have also suggested some plants which are difficult to obtain, but for which a wait is worthwhile as they are so perfect for their picture.

The connecting or tying in of one section of the garden with another, as illustrated in the backyard of Plan 2, is not usually necessary in small gardens, but is a relevant design principle for use in larger gardens where each vista is longer and broader and often needs to be correlated with the next. In small gardens which are divided into many pictures, some of which may be hedged-in by peninsulas of shrubs, the ground plants can be used as connectors. For example if a perennial is massed in one picture, a plant or two of it could be used in the adjacent section provided that this does not cause (what you consider to be) a clash of colours. Self-seeding annuals which stray from their allotted space will also serve to pull the whole design together if a few of these are allowed to remain where they self-seed.

Each of the plans depicts either the front yard or the backyard of a 16 m by 36 m suburban house block, south-facing, with a four bedroom family home, on soil which is neutral to slightly acidic. It was not possible within these pages to show example plans for varying sizes and shapes of land and houses, all aspects and all soil conditions. These sample plans are intended principally as a guide to picture-planned garden designing. I hope that they illustrate clearly the idea of drawing an overall plan for the garden and then picture-planning within that design. I suggest that before using any of the pictures included here, and in fact before buying plants for any picture, you ascertain whether or not the plants suggested will flower simultaneously in your area.

The scale throughout is 1 : 100.

PLAN 1

Front yard pictures

To suit frost-free, temperate to subtropical areas such as suburban Sydney and the coast of New South Wales.

Gardeners in many of Sydney's suburbs will find that by the time the trees and shrubs are providing wind protection and cover, summer humidity within the garden will have increased, allowing the inclusion of tropical ground plants.

Picture 1

TREES:	*Lagerstroemia indica* (pink crepe myrtle)
BOUNDARY SHRUBS:	*Escallonia* x *exoniensis* (pink escallonia)
PENINSULA:	*Jacobinia carnea*
GROUND PLANTS:	*Begonia scharfii* (or other pale pink species)
PICTURE:	a harmony of soft and deep pinks in summer
SECONDARY:	the beautiful shades of the lagerstroemia foliage in autumn is highlighted by the variety of dark greens in the leaves of the shrubs.

Picture 2

TREE:	*Prunus* x *yedoensis* (Yoshino cherry)
BOUNDARY SHRUBS:	*Camellia japonica*, pale pink of your choice
PENINSULA:	*Bouvardia humboldtii*
GROUND PLANTS:	pink violets and small ferns
PICTURE:	in late winter the pinkish-white blossom floats above the pale pink camellias and the deeper pink of the violets nestling among the ferns.
SECONDARY:	all year the foliage of the ferns provides an eye-catching contrast against that of the camellias.

Picture 3

TREES:	*Pistacia chinensis* (pistachio—not the nut-bearing one)
BOUNDARY SHRUBS:	*Ceratopetalum gummiferum* (Christmas bush)
GROUND PLANTS:	*Aquilegia canadensis, A. skinneri, Schizostylis coccinea* (Kaffir lily), *Lilium candidum* (madonna lily)
PICTURE:	the scarlet schizostylis provide a startling effect in autumn beneath the brilliant foliage of the pistachios. The bright red bracts of the Christmas bush may sometimes last to join in this display.
SECONDARY:	in mid- to late-spring the aquilegia species become a sea of soft-yellow to deep red, broken only by the budded spikes of the lilies. In summer the white Christmas bush blooms briefly accentuating the stately lilies, and then the bracts gradually deepen to red in the heat of the sun.

Picture 4

TREES:	*Sapium sebiferum*, Chinese tallow tree
BOUNDARY SHRUBS:	*Myrtus communis*, common myrtle
BACKGROUND SHRUBS:	white hydrangeas, for example *H. paniculata*
GROUND PLANTS:	*Helleborus orientalis* (Lenten rose) among the hydrangeas, *Acanthus mollis* (bear's breeches) (a few only for they are garden robbers), *Bletilla striata* (Chinese ground orchid) in the foreground.
PICTURE:	in early summer a lovely white and rosy-mauve scheme is provided by the myrtle and hydrangea blooms, the stately spikes of acanthus and the lower but equally attractive ones of the bletillas.
SECONDARY:	in autumn the sapiums assume beautiful colours, complemented by the autumn tints of the hydrangea flowers and foliage.

Picture 5

TREES:	as in picture 4
PENINSULA:	*Luculia gratissima* (with some acanthus in front of them, to hide their legginess)
GROUND PLANTS:	as in picture 4

Front yard of plan 1

PICTURE:	in winter the large, clear pink luculia blooms are lovely with the ground cover of greenish-white to deep pink hellebores, provided that any of these which are of undesirable shades are removed.
SECONDARY:	this section of garden provides striking foliage effects all year, the star in this regard being the acanthus.

Picture 6

TREES:	*Magnolia* x *soulangeana*
PENINSULA:	*Plectranthus ecklonii*
GROUND PLANTS:	*Hyacinthoides non-scripta* (pink only), *Galtonia candicans*, *Aconitum napellus* (monkshood), *Campanula rotundifolia* (harebell) or *C. persicifolia* (peach-leaf bellflower)
PICTURE:	the woodbells become a haze of pink beneath the firm pink and white magnolia blooms—a lovely contrast of shape and texture.

Picture 7

PICTURE:	in summer this area becomes a sheet of purple-blue from the plectranthus and the perennials, punctuated by the elegant spikes of white galtonia bells.

Picture 8

SHRUBS:	*Gardenia jasminoides* 'Florida'
GROUND PLANTS:	*Cyclamen hederifolium* (*C. neapolitanum*)
PICTURE:	this is a sea of pink cyclamen beneath the white gardenias in late summer and autumn.
SECONDARY:	attractive ground cover of silver-marbled cyclamen foliage features from March until December.

Backyard pictures

Picture 1

TREES: *Jacaranda acutifolia* (*J. mimosifolia*)

GROUND PLANTS: *Aurinia saxatilis* (*Alyssum saxatile*), *Tulbaghia violacea*

CLIMBERS: *Lonicera periclymenum* 'Serotina' (late Dutch honeysuckle) climbing through the jacarandas

PICTURE: mauvish-purple jacarandas, mauve tulbaghias and gold aurinias combine in bloom in mid- to late-spring. (Annual mulching with compost is necessary to maintain ground plants beneath jacarandas. Remove low branches when young to allow extra light to reach the aurinias, and to allow yourselves headroom in the outdoor-living area.)

SECONDARY: in autumn the honeysuckle produces dark purple and yellow flowers fading to mauve, complemented by mauve flowers of tulbaghia, which blooms for eight months.

Picture 2

TREES: *Prunus persica* 'Alboplena' (double white flowering peach)

PENINSULA: pink azalea of your choice (to flower with the prunus)

GROUND PLANTS: *Dicentra eximia* 'Bountiful', *Zephyranthes candida* (in the foreground)

PICTURE: a spring symphony of pink azaleas and dicentras beneath the beautiful white blossom

SECONDARY: the zephyranthes produce masses of white, yellow-throated flowers beneath the soft-toned autumn foliage of the prunuses.

Picture 3

TREES: *Diospyros kaki* (Japanese persimmon)

PENINSULA: *Streptosolen jamesonii* (orange browallia)

GROUND PLANTS: *Mimulus aurantiacus* (bush monkey flower)

PICTURE: orange and soft orange-buff tones from late spring until early autumn, complemented by the cestrums in picture 5

SECONDARY: brilliant autumn foliage of the persimmons, softened by the last flowers of the browallias and the cestrums.

Picture 4

TREES: *Ulmus procera* 'Vanhouttei' (golden elm)

BACKGROUND SHRUBS: *Dombeya natalensis* (cape wedding flower)

PENINSULA: *Beloperone guttata* 'Lutea' (yellow shrimp plant)

GROUND PLANTS: *Alchemilla mollis* (lady's mantle)

PICTURE: in summer yellowish-green is the predominant colour in the bracts of the beloperones, the frothy flower heads of the alchemillas and the mid-season foliage of the elms, all being highlighted by the dark dombeya foliage. The contrast in this picture is not in colour, but in shape and texture.

SECONDARY: in winter the dombeyas emerge from their background role to display their perfumed white flowers. The soft grey-green foliage of the alchemillas and the bracts of the beloperones contribute in a most satisfying way.

Picture 5

TREES: *Ulmus pumila* var. *arborea*, turkestan elm (the semi-evergreen *U. parvifolia* is not as suitable for your purpose. Purchase in winter to be sure you have the deciduous one)

PENINSULA: *Cestrum aurantiacum*

GROUND PLANTS: *Astilbe* x 'Mont Blanc' or *A.* x *arendsii* 'Deutschland' (these may be interplanted with early-flowering bulbs)

PICTURE: the feathery, creamy-white astilbe blooms are charming in summer massed in front of the golden-orange cestrums.

SECONDARY: the soft golden-apricot foliage which the elms produce in some years is perfect above the cestrums, still flowering in autumn.

Picture 6

TREES: as in picture 5

SHRUBS: as in picture 5

GROUND PLANTS: *Anemone hybrida* var. *alba* (*A. japonica*) (these can be interplanted with winter-

Backyard of plan 1

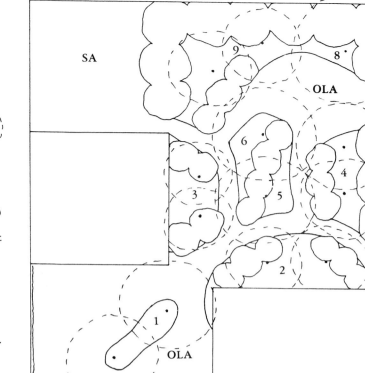

growing bulbs)

PICTURE:	the anemones' pure white blooms with prominent golden stamens are wonderful companions in autumn for the cestrums and the elms.

Picture 7

CLIMBERS:	*Clematis nepaulensis* (dormant for a short time in summer)
SHRUBS:	*Euphorbia wulfenii*
PICTURE:	for months during winter the greenish-cream clematis bells hang above the yellowish-green heads of the euphorbias, providing an interesting effect.
SECONDARY:	later in the season the fluffy white seed-heads above the blue-green euphorbia foliage is a pleasant sight.

Picture 8

TREE:	*Celtis sinensis* (Portuguese elm)
BACKGROUND SHRUBS:	*Telopea speciosissima* (New South Wales waratah)
GROUND PLANTS:	*Ceratostigma willmottianum, Geranium ibericum* or *G. pratense* in a good clear blue
PICTURE:	the deep blue flowers of ceratostigma and the paler shade of the geranium is a wonderful combination, giving pleasure all through the summer (provided that your geranium is not a form which hints at purple or reddish shades of blue).
SECONDARY:	the waratahs on their own are a picture in their spring season. In autumn the coloured foliage of both the celtis and the ceratostigma makes a good show, albeit an unusual one, for it is combined with the latter's blue flowers.

Picture 9

TREES:	*Malus* 'Aldenhamensis'
BACKGROUND SHRUBS:	*Ceonothus impressus* (or a hybrid which flowers with the malus)
PENINSULA:	*Leptospermum* 'Ruby Glow' or *L.* 'Ruby D' (tea-tree)
GROUND PLANTS:	*Myosotis alpestris* (forget-me-not)
PICTURE:	in mid-spring the malus and the leptospermum both have flowers of burgundy-pink and foliage of a deeper hue. The deep blue flowers of the ceonothus in the background and the sea of paler blue forget-me-nots below complete a most appealing picture.

PLAN 2

To suit Melbourne and much of southern Victoria. The dense planting, as illustrated in the backyard plan, to protect the garden from the worst effects of the hot, dry north-west wind, enables the inclusion of plants which would otherwise be dessicated. The pictures shown in the front yard are only suitable for this southerly aspect or for an easterly aspect.

Front yard pictures

Picture 1

TREE: *Prunus serrulata* 'Ukon' (the green cherry)
BOUNDARY SHRUBS: *Garrya elliptica* 'James Roof'
PENINSULA: *Euonymus alatus* (winged spindle bush)
GROUND PLANTS: *Helleborus argutifolius* (*H. corsicus*) (Corsican hellebore), *Tellima grandiflora*
PICTURE: in early spring this wonderful prunus opens its double, cream-splashed-green blossom, which lasts for four weeks, becoming tinged with pink as it ages. Flowering simultaneously beneath it are the greenish-cream hellebores and the tellimas, also greenish-cream and tinged with pink. The beautiful foliage of the latter is pinkish-burgundy, contrasting well with the light green leaves of the hellebore and the euonymus. This picture is perfectly set off by the dark green foliage of the garryas.
SECONDARY: the burgundy and pink autumn tones of the prunus, euonymus and tellima give way to a splendid show during winter of the large bunches of hellebore blooms and the long greenish-cream catkins of the garryas.

Picture 2

TREES: *Prunus mume* 'Alboplena' or *P.m.* 'Roseoplena' (flowering apricot)
BACKGROUND SHRUBS: *Viburnum tinus*
PENINSULA: *Rhododendron* 'Christmas Cheer'
GROUND PLANTS: pink and white violets (in the centre of the bed, interplanted with shade-tolerant spring-flowering bulbs), *Cyclamen coum* (massed in the foreground)
PICTURE: brightening the darkest of winter days, this pretty pink and white picture shows each of the contributing plants at its very best.
SECONDARY: in autumn the pinkish foliage of the prunuses is highlighted by the crimson-purple of the acer in picture 3.

Picture 3

TREE: *Acer palmatum* 'Atropurpureum' or *A.p.* 'Heptolobum Rubrum' (purple Japanese maple)
PENINSULA: *Abelia* x *grandiflora*
GROUND PLANTS: *Ajuga rubra* (red bugle), *Anthemis biebersteinii*
PICTURE: this is an all-year-round display of burgundy, white and silver. Even when the rich crimson-purple autumn foliage of the acer has fallen, the abelia leaves colour to take its place. From spring until autumn the abelia's white flowers are replaced by deep crimson bracts, and all the while the ground plants weave a silver and burgundy tapestry below.
SECONDARY: the bright yellow flowers of the anthemis introduce a startling contrast in their late-spring to summer season.

Picture 4

TREE: *Fraxinus oxycarpa* 'Raywoodii' (claret ash) with the lower branches removed
BOUNDARY SHRUBS: *Corylus maxima* 'Purpurea' (purple-leaf filbert), *Philadelphus coronarius* 'Aureus' (between the corylus)
BACKGROUND SHRUBS: *Hydrangea paniculata* var. *grandiflora*
GROUND PLANTS: *Hosta ventricosa*, *Helleborus orientalis* (Lenten rose), *Cyclamen hederifolium* (*C. neapolitanum*) in the foreground
PICTURE: this area presents a parade of pictures, each one heralding the arrival of a new season. At the beginning of summer the hydrangeas begin to produce their long white blooms, reaching their peak in January when the spikes of graceful, deep

Front yard of plan 2

Deciduous tree showing expected ultimate spread.

Deciduous shrub showing expected ultimate spread.

Evergreen shrub or tree showing expected ultimate spread.

Peninsula or group of shrubs.

Climbing plants on fences, walls or trellis.

Service area which can include garden shed, clothes-line, compost and rubbish bins and vegetable garden. **SA**

Outdoor-living area which can include table, seating and barbecue facilities. **OLA**

Main paths within the garden.

Access tracks or secondary paths.

The number of the picture described in the notes following the plan. **9**

violet hosta bells reach up to join them. As autumn approaches the hydrangea blooms turn to pink and the cyclamens begin to flower without leaves. By mid-autumn their beautiful leaves carpet the ground beneath the mass of pink blooms, the pink of the hydrangea flowers deepens and the claret ash turns ruby. As winter sets in the hellebores shake off their blanket of leaves and emerge into their winter starring role, retreating again as the corylus and philadelphus break into leaf to produce the best purple and gold foliage display of all. By the time their leaves lose their brilliance, the hydrangeas are beginning again.

Background pictures

The 'tying in' of the garden, connecting one section with another, as illustrated in this plan, is usually not necessary in small gardens. It is shown here as an example of this design principle.

Picture 1

TREE: *Magnolia denudata* (yulan)

BACKGROUND SHRUBS: these also form the peninsula; *Thuya occidentalis* 'Fastigiata' (green column thuya) (not *T. plicata* 'Fastigiata') or *Cupressus sempervirons* var. *stricta*

SHRUBS: *Spiraea* x *bumalda* 'Anthony Waterer' (one at each end of the picture)

GROUND PLANTS: *Symphoricarpus rivularis* (*S. albus*) (snowberry) in the dense shade, *Nerine bowdenii* (pink nerine) in groups towards the front, *Rhodohypoxis baurii* in the sunniest places at the front interspersed with a few plants of *Francoa ramosa* (bridal wreath)

PICTURE: in late winter or very early spring, the magnolia displays on its leafless skeleton the large, pure-white, perfumed blooms, which are strikingly conspicuous against the dark green foliage of the thuyas. This is a simple but most effective picture.

SECONDARY: summer colour is provided by the small, pink snowberry bells, the large heads of crimson spiraea flowers and the rhodohypoxis. The spikes of francoa flowers are white blotched with crimson, blending in this picture and tying-in with picture 2. In autumn the deep pink nerines are lovely with a backdrop of the snow-white berries of the symphoricarpus, which hold on the bushes well into winter.

Picture 2

SHRUBS: *Rosa rugosa* 'Frau Dagmar Hastrup' (in the centre), *Rosa* 'The Fairy' (one at each end)

GROUND PLANTS: *Gypsophila repens* var. *rosea*, to the front, interspersed with *Francoa ramosa* (bridal wreath). (These ground plants can be interplanted with early-flowering, winter-growing bulbs.)

PICTURE: this cottage picture is a harmony of soft pinks throughout the summer and autumn.

SECONDARY: in the winter the rugosa rose dazzles with its large crimson fruits, and the francoa foliage turns to deep crimson below.

Picture 3

TREE: *Malus ioensis* var. *plena* (betchel crab)

PENINSULA: *Myrtus communis* (common myrtle)

GROUND PLANTS: *Triteleia lineata* var. *rosea*, *Heuchera* x *brizoides* in a pale pink form (in the foreground)

PICTURE: in mid-spring the malus produces its large, pink-and-white double flowers accompanied by the tall spikes of pink triteleia and the first sprays of the heuchera, highlighted by the dark backdrop of the myrtles.

SECONDARY: by mid-summer the myrtles are covered with large, perfumed white blooms complemented by the full, soft-pink sprays of the heuchera. The malus is delightful in autumn, producing the full range of autumn colour in its foliage.

Picture 4

TREE: *Laburnum* x *watereri* 'Vossii'

PENINSULA: *Pittosporum tenuifolium* 'Tom Thumb'

GROUND PLANTS: *Convallaria majalis* (lily of the valley)

PICTURE: the golden chains of the laburnum are accentuated by the burgundy-black foliage of the pittosporums and the prunuses (in picture 5). In most years the lily of the valley will flower simultaneously with this late spring picture.

SECONDARY: the grouping of dwarf pittosporums creates all-year-round interest as its bright, light-green young growth changes to shiny burgundy-black at maturity.

Backyard of plan 2

KEY

Deciduous tree
showing expected
ultimate spread.

Deciduous shrub
showing expected
ultimate spread.

Evergreen shrub or
tree showing
expected ultimate
spread.

Peninsula or group of
shrubs.

Climbing plants on
fences, walls or
trellis.

Service area which
can include garden
shed, clothes-line,
compost and rubbish
bins and vegetable
garden.

SA

Outdoor-living area
which can include
table, seating and
barbecue facilities.

OLA

Main paths within
the garden.

Access tracks or
secondary paths.

The number of the
picture described in
the notes following
the plan.

9

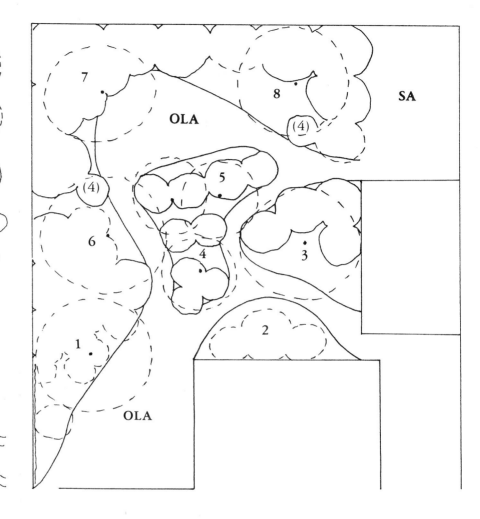

Picture 5

TREES:	*Prunus cerasifera* 'Nigra'
SHRUBS:	*Rhododendron* 'Cilpinense'
GROUND PLANTS:	*Chrysanthemum ptarmicaeflorum*, *Sedum spathufolium* 'Purpureum' or *Polygonum capitatum* in a good burgundy-leaved form. (Either of these could be interplanted with early-flowering bulbs.)
PICTURE:	the delicate, single, pink blossom of the prunuses stands out against the burgundy-black foliage in early spring, and, underneath, the pink rhododendron combines prettily.
SECONDARY:	viewed from the secluded outdoor-living area, this section of the garden is a picture from early spring until mid-winter, for the silvery-white, lacy foliage of the chrysanthemum is striking against the dark foliage of the prunuses, which fades to deep burgundy by mid-summer. The interesting silver and burgundy foliage of the sedum in the foreground picks up the colours of its companions charmingly. (Many people choose to cut off the large, white flowers of the chrysanthemum, using it purely as a foliage plant and keeping it compact in this way.)

Picture 6

TREE: *Ulmus procera* 'Variegatum' (silver elm)

BACKGROUND SHRUBS: as in picture 1

SHRUBS: *Viburnum carlesii* (Korean viburnum), *Pittosporum tenuifolium* 'Tom Thumb' (one only, to tie this section of the garden in with picture 4)

GROUND PLANTS: *Erythronium dens-canis* 'Rose Queen' (dog's tooth violet), *Cyclamen persicum* in the foreground

PICTURE: in early spring the viburnum opens its sweetest-scented white flowers from pink buds, while below the charming erythroniums nod their heads above the carpet of pink cyclamen blooms.

SECONDARY: the beautiful leaves of the silver elm, pale green speckled with cream and white, stand out well against the background shrubs and pick up the similar colour in the leaves of the pittosporum in picture 7.

Picture 7

TREE: *Cratageus pubescens* (Mexican hawthorn)

BACKGROUND TREES: *Arbutus unedo* (strawberry tree), *Pittosporum eugenioides* 'Variegatum' (silver tarata) (one only in the corner between the arbutus)

SHRUBS: *Pieris japonica* 'Variegatum', *Camellia japonica* 'Flame' in between the two pierises

GROUND PLANTS: *Leucojum aestivum* (snowflake), *Nierembergia rivularis*, *Viola tricolor* (johnny-jump-up)

PICTURE: an attractive late-winter picture is provided by the flame-red camellia massed beneath with the white-tipped-green snowflakes and flanked by the graceful sprays of white pieris bells. The snowflakes are accentuated by the dark, glossy camellia foliage, which is in turn highlighted by the pale, variegated pittosporum foliage. Conversely, the pretty pale green and white foliage of the pieris stands out well against the dark arbutus leaves. The pittosporum, commonly-grown but rarely used effectively, is strikingly beautiful all year flanked by the arbutus with the camellia in the foreground.

SECONDARY: in autumn many of the cratageus leaves turn orange and red, and the large berries ripen to bright yellow, holding on the tree well into winter while the strawberry-like fruits of the arbutus turn from yellow to deep red. A pretty effect is created in summer by the gay little johnny-jump-ups flowering above the large white saucers of the nierembergia.

Picture 8

TREE: *Catalpa bignonioides* (Indian bean tree)

BACKGROUND SHRUBS: *Buddleia fallowiana* if available or *B. davidii* in a lavender or lilac shade, *Cytisus battandierii* 'Yellow Tail' (Morocco broom), one at each end.

SHRUB: *Pittosporum tenuifolium* 'Tom Thumb', one only to tie this section of the garden in with the rest

GROUND PLANTS: *Campanula portenschlagiana*, *Lilium pumilum* 'Golden Splendour' or another yellow-flowered lily

PICTURE: the purple and yellow markings on the white flowers of the catalpa are highlighted by the shrubs and ground plants behind and beneath it, which during summer display a delightful combination of mauve, lavender and yellow.

SECONDARY: the white, woolly leaves of the buddleias and the silvery-grey ones of the cytisus provide a backdrop which is refreshingly different from the usual dark greens.

PLAN 3

Front yard pictures

To suit areas with cold winters and mild to warm summers, such as Canberra, much of Tasmania, north-eastern Victoria, and the hills adjacent to Sydney, Melbourne and Adelaide.

Some of the cool, mountainous areas within this climatic zone are relatively frost-free, and gardeners with this advantage can be more adventuresome where frost-tender plants are concerned.

Picture 1

SHRUBS: *Pieris formosa* var. *forrestii*, *Camellia japonica* 'Flame', *Rhododendron indicum* (*Azalea indica*) 'Leapold Astrid'

PICTURE: a red and white setting to brighten the late-winter days; the long, white panicles of honey-scented pieris bells appear among the bright red new growth, joined by the deep scarlet camellia blooms and the azaleas, white with a dark red frill.

Picture 2

TREE: *Pistacia chinensis* (Chinese pistachio)

BACKGROUND SHRUBS: *Cotinus coggygria* 'Folliis Purpureis' (purple-leaved smoke-bush)

PENINSULAS: *Kalmia latifolia* (mountain laurel), *Chrysanthemum frutescens* 'Pink Beauty' or *C.f.* 'Roseo-plena' (double pink marguerite) on the corner

GROUND PLANTS: *Heuchera* x *brizoides*, pale pink form (in the foreground), *Thalictrum aquilegiifolium* (meadow rue)

PICTURE: in late spring the beautiful kalmia flowers and the soft pink marguerites (pruned in winter to promote spring and summer flowering) are brought sharply into focus by the haze around them, created by the pink heucheras below, the deeper, mauvish-pink thalictrums behind and the plum-red flower sprays of the cotinus overhead.

SECONDARY: the brilliant red autumn foliage of the pistacia is softened by the more subdued tints of cotinuses creating a wonderful foliage display.

Picture 3

TREE: *Davidia involucrata* (dove tree)

BACKGROUND SHRUBS: *Garrya elliptica* 'James Roof' (catkin bush), *Pittosporum eugenioides* 'Variegatum' (silver tarata) between the garryas

GROUND PLANTS: *Viola cornuta* 'Northfield Gem' or other good blue-violet form, *Nierembergia rivularis*

PICTURE: in mid-spring the large, white bracts of the davidia float above a carpet of the violas, creating a breathtaking display.

SECONDARY: the violas continue to bloom for many months, teaming up in summer with the white saucers of the nierembergias. In winter when the deciduous plants are dormant, the pittosporum and the garryas emerge to put on a wonderful show. The pale pittosporum foliage gleams beneath dull skies, accentuated by the matt, dark-green leaves of the garryas, and the long, greenish-cream catkins are seen at their very best in this setting.

Picture 4

SHRUBS: *Chrysanthemum ptarmicaeflorum*, *C. frutescens* 'Pink Beauty' or *C.f.* 'Roseo-plena' (double pink marguerite)

GROUND PLANTS: *Acanthus spinosus* (bear's breeches) between the chrysanthemums

PICTURE: beautiful all year for its startling foliage contrasts, this area is at its peak in summer when the bold spikes of acanthus blooms pick up the pink of the marguerites (pruned as suggested in picture 2) and the silvery-white of the chrysanthemum.

SECONDARY: the marguerite ties this section of the garden in with picture 2, thus pulling the whole design together. It flowers all year except for a short time after pruning, and always looks good with the glossy dark-green of the large acanthus leaves and the feathery, silver chrysanthemum foliage.

Front yard of plan 3

Picture 5

TREES:	*Prunus subhirtella* 'Autumnalis' (winter cherry)
BACKGROUND SHRUBS:	*Brachyglottis repanda* 'Purpurea' (purple rangiora)
PENINSULA:	*Fuchsia magellanica* (lady's eardrops)
GROUND PLANTS:	*Cyclamen hederifolium* (*C. neapolitanum*), *C. coum*, *Galanthus nivalis* (snowdrop)
PICTURE:	this amazing little prunus produces its delicate white blossom for five months from late autumn until early spring. In the autumn it is lovely with a carpet at its feet of *Cyclamen hederifolium*, from which *C. coum* takes over in the winter. In late winter the pearly-white snowdrops pierce the rose-pink carpet, and through all these months the white blossom is strikingly highlighted by the large leaves of the brachyglottis, black-purple with a silvery-white underside, and the deep crimson blooms of the fuchsia.
SECONDARY:	the brachyglottis produces large sprays of heavily-scented, delicate purple flowers in late spring, echoing the purple corollas of the fuchsias.

Picture 6

TREE:	*Acer japonicum* 'Aureum' (golden full moon maple)
BACKGROUND SHRUBS:	as in picture 5
PENINSULA:	*Pittosporum tenuifolium* 'Tom Thumb'
GROUND PLANTS:	*Francoa ramosa* (bridal wreath)
PICTURE:	in spring the soft yellow foliage of the acer is dazzling against the black-purple leaves of the brachyglottis and the pittosporum. Later the acer foliage becomes pale lime-green, matched by the new growth of the pittosporum.
SECONDARY:	the spikes of delicate francoa blooms, white with burgundy markings, are charming in summer in this setting, and their handsome leaves provide good ground cover all year.

Backyard pictures

Picture 1

TREE: *Catalpa bignonioides* 'Aurea' (golden catalpa) with lower branches removed

BACKGROUND SHRUBS: *Corylopsis willmottiae* 'Spring Purple'

GROUND PLANTS: *Anemone blanda* (Grecian windflower), *Campanula persicifolia* (peach-leaf bellflower)

PICTURE: in late winter or early spring the corylopsis produce dense racemes of fragrant yellow flowers accompanied in the foreground by the blue, yellow-centred anemones.

SECONDARY: when the anemones become dormant the campanulas emerge to send up their spikes of purple bells, harmonizing with the catalpa blooms of white marked with yellow and purple. The plum-purple young leaves of the corylopsis and the burnished gold ones of the catalpa combine to create a very beautiful foliage effect for months.

Picture 2

TREES: *Cornus kousa* var. *chinensis*, *Acer palmatum* 'Seiryu'

PENINSULA: *Cotinus coggygria* 'Flame'

GROUND PLANTS: *Filipendula hexapetala* 'Flore-pleno' (meadowsweet) in the background beneath the cotinus, *Corydalis ochroleuca* in the foreground, *Convallaria majalis* (lily of the valley) in the background beneath the acer, *Gentiana acaulis* in the foreground

PICTURE: in the early summer the large, cream bracts of the dogwood combine beautifully with the cream blooms of the filipendula and the corydalis, and the hint of pink in the buds of the former is enlivened by the fluffy pink flower sprays of the cotinus.

SECONDARY: this area contains a pleasant combination of foliage shapes and textures; broad, dull green, wavy-edged cornus leaves, finely dissected and lacy on the acer, slender-stalked and round cotinus foliage, fresh-green and feathery filipendula, and grey and fern-like corydalis. The scene is a blaze of bronze, crimson, deep red and irridescent orange as the trees and shrubs assume their autumn tints. A spectacular spring scene is provided by the carpet of royal-blue gentian trumpets in front of the massed spikes of white lily of the valley.

Picture 3

TREES: *Pterostyrax hispida* (epaulette tree)

BACKGROUND SHRUBS: (on the fence-line) *Rhododendron augustinii* 'Electra'

PENINSULA: as above

GROUND PLANTS: *Primula vulgaris* (English primrose) in the background towards the pterostyrax,

PICTURE: *Convolvulus mauritanicus* in the foreground. These can be interplanted with early-flowering bulbs

SECONDARY: a simple but effective early summer picture, achieved with a carpet of the blue-mauve convolvulus beneath the pretty white chains of the pterostyrax.
in spring the luminous blue-violet rhododendrons are charming with the lemon primroses.

Picture 4

TREE: *Fagus sylvatica* 'Riversii' (purple beech)

BACKGROUND SHRUBS: *Philadelphus coronarius* 'Aureus' (golden mock orange)

GROUND PLANTS: *Chamaecyparispericlymenum canadensis* (creeping dogwood) in the background, *Cyclamen purpurascens* (*C. europaeum*) (summer cyclamen), *C. hederifolium* (*C. neapolitanum*) (autumn cyclamen), *C. coum* (winter cyclamen)

PICTURE: another example of a striking gold and purple foliage effect, this time provided by the large, glossy, purple leaves of the beech and the soft, matt, bright yellow leaves of the philadelphus. This picture is enhanced in late spring by the creamy-white scented flowers of the philadelphus and the large, white bracts of the cornus.

SECONDARY: throughout the summer, autumn and winter the cyclamens (one of the few plants which will grow well beneath a beech) flower in succession above their attractive foliage.

Picture 5

TREES:	*Stewartia pseudocamellia*
BACKGROUND SHRUBS:	*Abutilon* x *suntense* 'Jermyns' or *Abutilon vitifolium* 'Veronica Tennant'
PENINSULA:	*Rhododendron fragrans*
GROUND PLANTS:	*Campanula garganica*
PICTURE:	the abutilons produce their mauve flowers for many months, being joined in early summer by the pale mauve, fragrant rhododendrons and later by the elegant wands of blue-mauve campanulas and the white camellia-like stewartia blooms.
SECONDARY:	the leaves of the stewartias become yellow and red in autumn, and then fall to reveal the interesting, flaking bark against the backdrop of the grey, felted abutilon leaves.

Picture 6

BACKGROUND TREES:	*Embothrium coccineum* or *E.c.* var. *lanceolatum*, (Chilean fire bush), *Elaeocarpus dentatus* in the corner between the embothriums
GROUND PLANTS:	*Aconitum napellus* (monkshood) can be interplanted with early-flowering bulbs
PICTURE:	a spectacular spring display provided by the dark red embothriums and the pure-white, fringed elaeocarpus flowers.
SECONDARY:	in summer and autumn the tall spires of deep, purple-blue aconitum flowers combine well with the berries of the elaeocarpus.

Picture 7

TREE:	*Oxydendrum arboreum* (sorrel tree)
BACKGROUND SHRUBS:	*Hydrangea quercifolia* (oak leaf hydrangea)
GROUND PLANTS:	*Lamium maculatum*
PICTURE:	the large sprays of white oxydendrum flowers are lovely in late summer above the hydrangeas. These are white, tinted pink and purple, combining well with the lamium, which provides good all-year-round ground cover.
SECONDARY:	the oxydendrum and the hydrangeas both produce excellent autumn colour.

Picture 8

TREES:	*Malus* 'Profusion' or *M.* x *eleyii* (purple crab)
CLIMBERS:	*Rosa* 'Zephirine Drouhin' allowed to scramble through the trees
BACKGROUND TREES:	*Pittosporum tenuifolium* (Kohuhu) in the corner
BACKGROUND SHRUBS:	*Viburnum* x *burkwoodii*, *Eucryphia glutinosa* (one at each end of this picture)
GROUND PLANTS:	*Myosotis alpestris* (forget-me-not), *Aquilegia vulgaris* (granny's bonnet), *Digitalis purpurea* (foxglove), *Nigella damascena* (love-in-a-mist), *Watsonia beatricis*, *Lilium regale*, *Nerine bowdenii*, *Viola tricolor* (johnny-jump-up)
PICTURE:	this is a 'secret' or wild garden entered at either end by pushing between a eucryphia and a philadelphus. The pale green pittosporum leaves light up this corner and there is nearly something in bloom all year. The viburnums flower from mid-winter until the dark blossom emerges on the maluses, wonderful with a sea of forget-me-nots below. The light-growing rambling roses cover the trees with flowers from mid-spring onwards and below there is a succession of flowers from the aquilegias, foxgloves, love-in-a-mist, watsonias, lilies, nerines and violas. In summer the eucryphias produce abundant white flowers and then colour quite prettily in autumn. Although not picture-planned, this corner has a charm of its own, and particularly appealing to children.

Backyard of plan 3

KEY

Deciduous tree
showing expected
ultimate spread.

Deciduous shrub
showing expected
ultimate spread.

Evergreen shrub or
tree showing
expected ultimate
spread.

Peninsula or group of
shrubs.

Climbing plants on
fences, walls or
trellis.

Service area which
can include garden
shed, clothes-line,
compost and rubbish
bins and vegetable
garden.

Outdoor-living area
which can include
table, seating and
barbecue facilities.

Main paths within
the garden.

Access tracks or
secondary paths.

The number of the
picture described in
the notes following
the plan.

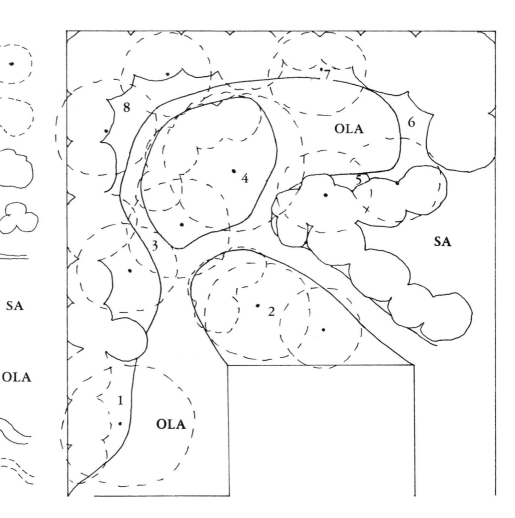

PLAN 4

To suit areas with cold winters and warm to hot summers, such as Adelaide and parts of southern South Australia and northern Victoria.

Gardeners in the frost-free areas of Adelaide and southern South Australia will be able to include some frost-tender plants initially, but gardeners in frost-prone areas, such as northern Victoria, are advised to wait until the garden is established before using plants which may be at risk.

Front yard pictures

Picture 1

SHRUBS:	*Cassia nemophila* var. *zygophylla* (*C. eremophylla*) (silver cassia)
GROUND PLANTS:	*Matricaria eximia* 'Golden Moss' (*Chrysanthemum parthenium*) (dwarf golden feverfew)
PICTURE:	all year the combination of the silver, fine-leaved foliage of the cassia and the golden foliage of the matricaria provide an interesting and pleasing contrast.
SECONDARY:	in spring this contrast of foliage colour and texture is accentuated dramatically by the golden flowers of the cassia.

Picture 2

TREE:	*Fraxinus oxycarpa* 'Raywoodii' (claret ash)
PENINSULA:	*Cistus* 'Silver Pink'
GROUND PLANTS:	*Epilobium angustifolium* (willow herb)
PICTURE:	in summer the soft silvery-pink of the large cistus blooms are 'lifted' by the deeper pink of the tall epilobium spikes. This show may last until the claret ash assumes its deep ruby-red tones overhead.
SECONDARY:	as autumn reaches its peak the dark shades of the claret ash contrast beautifully with the gold of the elm which in turn is highlighted by the dark green of the garryas.

Picture 3

TREE:	*Ulmus procera* 'Vanhouttei' (golden elm)
BOUNDARY SHRUBS:	*Garrya elliptica* 'James Roof'
GROUND PLANTS:	*Dictamnus albus* (burning bush) can be interplanted with winter-growing bulbs
PICTURE:	beneath the yellowish-green mid-summer foliage of the elms, the dictamnus sends up spikes of white blooms opening from yellowish-green buds. These are highlighted by the dark foliage of the garryas in the background.
SECONDARY:	in winter the garryas emerge to perform in their own starring role, covering their dark green foliage with long catkins of pale greenish-cream.

Picture 4

TREE:	*Magnolia stellata* (star magnolia)
CLIMBERS:	*Ampelopsis brevipedunculata* (turquoise berry vine)
GROUND PLANTS:	*Ipheion uniflora* 'Froyle Mill' (spring star flower), *Viola cornuta* (in a good purple-blue form)
PICTURE:	in early spring the ipheion is a carpet of deep violet-purple beneath the white magnolia blooms.
SECONDARY:	*Viola cornuta* flowers continuously throughout the spring and summer months until in late summer its charming blooms serve to highlight the bunches of blue and purple berries on the vine.

Picture 5

TREE:	*Viburnum opulus* 'Sterile' (snowball tree) with the lower branches removed
PENINSULA:	*Ceratostigma willmottianum*
GROUND PLANTS:	*Cynoglossum nervosum* can be interplanted with winter-growing bulbs
PICTURE:	a blue and white summer picture of white 'snowballs' above the deep blue flowers of the ceratostigma and the cynoglossum, with a backdrop of blue hydrangeas and glimpses of the lilies in picture 6.
SECONDARY:	the viburnum produces good dark red autumn colour above the red-tinted leaves

Deciduous tree
showing expected
ultimate spread.

Deciduous shrub
showing expected
ultimate spread.

Evergreen shrub or
tree showing
expected ultimate
spread.

Peninsula or group of
shrubs.

Climbing plants on
fences, walls or
trellis.

Service area which
can include garden
shed, clothes-line,
compost and rubbish
bins and vegetable
garden.   **SA**

Outdoor-living area
which can include
table, seating and   **OLA**
barbecue facilities.

Main paths within
the garden.

Access tracks or
secondary paths.

The number of the
picture described in   9
the notes following
the plan.

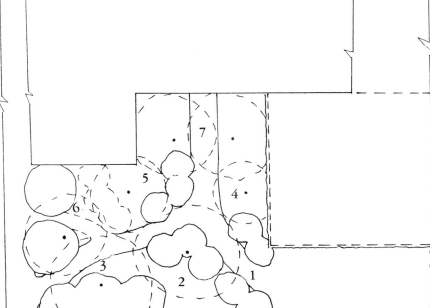

Front yard of plan 4

of the ceratostigma, offset in an unusual way by the last of the blue flowers and the grey cynoglossum foliage.

Picture 6

TREE:	as in picture 5
BOUNDARY SHRUBS:	*Viburnum tinus*
PENINSULA:	*Hydrangea macrophylla* (a good deep blue form if your soil is suitable) or *Ceonothus* 'Burkwoodii' (or other late-flowering form)
GROUND PLANTS:	*Helleborus orientalis* (Lenten rose) selected in white and plum or burgundy tones, *Lilium candidum* (madonna lily)
PICTURE:	in summer the stately white lilies and the white 'snowballs' provide an eye-catching contrast of shape and texture against the blue background of hydrangeas or ceonothus.
SECONDARY:	a lovely show is put on all winter by the white flowers of *Viburnum tinus* opening from burgundy buds, with these two colours echoed in the helleborus below.

Picture 7

TREES:	*Sorbus* spp. The correct tree for this picture, sold variously as *S. discolor*, *S. cashmirianus* and *S. hupehensis*, is narrow-growing with pink to burgundy autumn foliage and bunches of large berries which are white flushed pink. If purchased in autumn all three attributes can be checked, ensuring that you get the right sorbus no matter what it is called at the time.
GROUND PLANTS:	*Viola cornuta*, *Schizostylis coccinea* 'Viscountess Byng' (usually sold in this country as *S.c.* 'Mrs Hegarty'), *Convallaria majalis* (lily of the valley)
PICTURE:	in late spring and early summer the sorbus bears its white flowers, beneath which the white lily of the valley and the purple-blue violas jostle each other for space to show their lovely flowers.
SECONDARY:	an unusual autumn picture is created with the pink and burgundy foliage above the last of the viola blooms. After the foliage display is over the sorbus berries become more prominent, flushing with pride until they almost match the pink of the lovely spikes of schizostylis flowers below.

Backyard pictures

Picture 1

TREE: *Nyssa sylvatica* (tupelo)

BACKGROUND SHRUBS: *Buddleia salvifolia* (smoky buddleia)

GROUND PLANTS: *Chieranthus mutabilis* var. *variegatus* (perennial wallflower) can be interplanted with tall-growing bulbs such as liliums

PICTURE: in late winter or early spring the buddleia produces its large, fragrant plumes of smoky lilac flowers, and the wallflower begins its long flowering season by covering itself with lovely mauve-pink flowers.

SECONDARY: long after the buddleia retreats once more into its background role, the wallflower cheerfully blooms on and on, pausing for breath while the nyssa displays its brilliant autumn foliage. (In suitable situations the wallflower will actually flower all year.)

Picture 2

TREES: *Lagerstroemia indica* (pink crepe myrtle)

PENINSULA: *Acanthus spinosus*

GROUND PLANTS: *Sidalcea malviflora* (checkerbloom), *Prunella webbiana* 'Pink Loveliness' (in the foreground)

PICTURE: this area is at its best in summer when the flesh-pink crepe myrtle and the pink and grey acanthus are highlighted by the rosy-pink display of the sidalcea and the prunella.

SECONDARY: as the perennials complete their show in autumn, the lagerstroemias assume their autumn dress of orange.

Picture 3

TREE: *Quercus palustris* (pin oak)

PENINSULA: *Berberis* x *smithii* or *B. thunbergii* 'Atropurpurea'

GROUND PLANTS: *Senecio cineraria* (*Cineraria maritima*) (silver groundsel)

PICTURE: no matter from where it is viewed or at what time of year, this section of the garden displays excellent contrasts of foliage colour, shape and texture. The woolly silver foliage of the senecio is startling against both the large, glossy, dark green leaves of the acanthus and the smaller deep-red to coppery-purple ones of the berberis. The pin oak above varies its contribution to the scene from light green through darker greens and finally to orange or scarlet.

SECONDARY: the yellow flowers of the berberis and the senecio provide interesting but merely incidental contrasts in this foliage picture.

Picture 4

SHRUBS: *Podalyria sericea* (silky podalyria)

PICTURE: a charming mid-winter display of pink and grey is provided by the flowers and foliage of the podalyria.

SECONDARY: later the pink flowers are replaced by showy green seed pods, while the silky grey foliage is decorative all year.

Picture 5

TREE: *Metasequoia glyptostroboides* (dawn redwood)

BACKGROUND SHRUBS: *Dodonaea viscosa* 'Purpurea' (purple hopbush)

PENINSULAS: *Philadelphus coronaria* 'Aureus'

GROUND PLANTS: *Phygelius capensis* (cape fuchsia), *Solidago* x 'Golden Baby' (dwarf golden rod) in the foreground

PICTURE: in autumn the display in this area reaches its peak, for the golden rods and the soft orange fuchsias, which have been flowering for months, are now highlighted by the apricot foliage of the metasequoias.

SECONDARY: early spring foliage of shining bronze-purple, matt bright yellow and velvety lime-green on, respectively, the dodonaea, philadelphus and metasequoia provides a lovely picture in this corner of the garden.

Picture 6

TREES: *Malus* 'Lemoinei'

PENINSULA: *Polygala* 'Dalmaisiana' (*P.* 'Grandis')

Backyard of plan 4

KEY

Deciduous tree showing expected ultimate spread.

Deciduous shrub showing expected ultimate spread.

Evergreen shrub or tree showing expected ultimate spread.

Peninsula or group of shrubs.

Climbing plants on fences, walls or trellis.

Service area which can include garden shed, clothes-line, compost and rubbish bins and vegetable garden.

SA

Outdoor-living area which can include table, seating and barbecue facilities.

OLA

Main paths within the garden.

Access tracks or secondary paths.

The number of the picture described in the notes following the plan.

9

GROUND PLANTS:	*Erysimum* x *linifolium* (blister cress)
PICTURE:	the spring display of the rosy-purple polygala and the more subdued tones of the malus flowers and young leaves is softened by the lavender-pink of the erysimum.
SECONDARY:	the erysimum continues blooming throughout the summer and the polygala keeps on producing some blooms. A plant or two of *Acanthus mollis*, carefully placed, could add effectively to this summer scene, but remember to allow for its bad-mannered ways.

Picture 7

BACKGROUND SHRUBS:	*Cotinus coggygria* 'Folliis Purpureis' (purple-leaved smoke-bush)
FOREGROUND SHRUBS:	*Cistus crispus*
GROUND PLANTS:	*Penstemon davidsonii* (mountain pride)
PICTURE:	in summer this corner is transformed into a bright scene as the cotinus 'smokes' with pinkish-purple plumes, the cistus is smothered with its large cerise-pink saucers and the penstemon carpets the ground with similarly coloured trumpets.

Picture 8

TREE:	*Acer negundo* 'Variegatum' (*A. n. argenteum*) (ghost tree)
BACKGROUND SHRUBS:	*Philadelphus mexicanus*
GROUND PLANTS:	*Nierembergia rivularis* (*N. repens*) (can be interplanted with winter-growing bulbs), *Nigella damascena* (love-in-a-mist) (self-seeding annual)
PICTURE:	in early summer the philadelphus produces its large, creamy-white blooms accentuated by the white and green leaves of the acer, and the nierembergia and nigella produce their first flush of flowers.
SECONDARY:	throughout the summer months the nierembergia's white saucers and the clear-blue nigella blooms create a soft blue and white picture which is quite lovely.

PLAN 5

Front yard pictures

To suit subtropical areas, verging on tropical, such as Brisbane and the south Queensland coast.

Once the trees and shrubs are providing cover and wind-protection, humidity will be increased within the garden allowing the inclusion of many orchid species and rare tropical ground plants.

Picture 1

TREES:	*Cassia fistula* (golden shower)
BOUNDARY SHRUBS:	*Caesalpinia gilliesii* (bird of paradise)
CLIMBERS:	*Stigmaphyllon ciliata* (Brazilian glory vine)
PENINSULA:	*Allamanda neriifolia*
GROUND PLANTS:	*Chlidanthus fragrans, Phygelius capensis, Zephyranthes* spp. in shades of white, cream and yellow (in dense patches at the entrance to the path)
PICTURE:	this is a progressive picture beginning in early summer when the yellow and orange flowers of the shrubs are featuring with the cassias. The shrubs continue to bloom throughout summer and autumn while the bulbs, perennials and the climber on the carport each in their own season contribute to completing the picture.

Picture 2

TREES:	*Sapium sebiferum* (Chinese tallow tree)
BOUNDARY SHRUBS:	*Adhotoda vasica*
PENINSULA:	*Iboza riparia*
GROUND PLANTS:	*Hypoestes aristata* (velvet plant), *Dichorisandra thyrsiflora*
PICTURE:	in late winter and all through the spring this area is a pretty scene for the lavender flowers of the iboza and white and mauve adhotoda flowers are massed beneath by the pinkish mauve of the hypoestes.
SECONDARY:	in summer and autumn this area is illuminated by the vivid violet spikes of dichorisandra which are joined in their display by the autumn gold and claret of the sapiums.

Picture 3

GROUND PLANTS:	*Zephyranthes* spp. and *Habranthus* spp. in white and deep pink.
PICTURE:	these bulbs, thickly planted, make a welcoming show of pink and white at the entrance to the garden in late summer and early autumn.

Picture 4

TREE:	*Melia azedarach* var. *australasica* (white cedar)
BOUNDARY SHRUBS:	*Brunsvelsia latifolia*
PENINSULA:	*Mackaya bella*
GROUND PLANTS:	*Crinum pedunculatum* or *C. bulbispermum* (white)
PICTURE:	when the melia puts forth its lilac flowers in late spring, the lavender-blue brunsvelsia, the delicate pale-lilac mackaya and the white crinums join it in bloom to complete the picture.
SECONDARY:	the orange-yellow berries of the melia brighten the winter scene in the garden.

Picture 5

TREE:	*Peltophorum inerme* (yellow poinciana)
BACKGROUND SHRUBS:	*Codiaeum variegatum* (croton) in its cream and yellow forms
PENINSULA:	*Plumeria rubra* 'Acutifolia' (frangipani)
GROUND PLANTS:	*Heterocentron roseum* (*Heeria rosea*)
PICTURE:	for months from early summer until late autumn the cream and yellow frangipani flowers are in perfect harmony with the similarly coloured croton foliage, thrown into relief by the dense green foliage of the heterocentron. In mid-summer the yellow throats of the frangipani are highlighted by the yellow blooms of the tree overhead.
SECONDARY:	as the frangipani is finishing, the heterocentron begins its floral display, bearing its cerise heads of bloom until late winter, creating a fascinating effect below the striking smoky seed pods of the peltophorum.

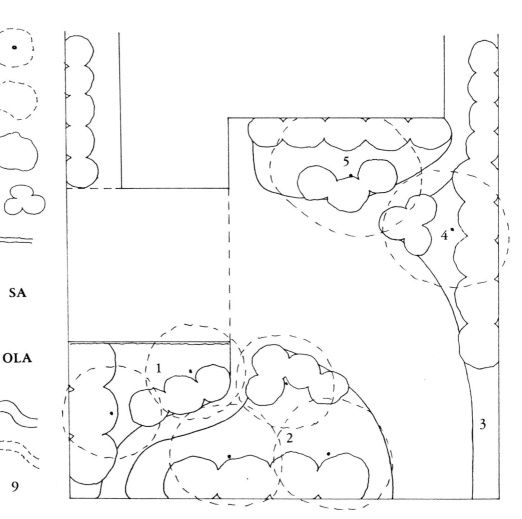

Front yard of plan 5

Deciduous tree
showing expected
ultimate spread.

Deciduous shrub
showing expected
ultimate spread.

Evergreen shrub or
tree showing
expected ultimate
spread.

Peninsula or group of
shrubs.

Climbing plants on
fences, walls or
trellis.

Service area which
can include garden
shed, clothes-line,
compost and rubbish
bins and vegetable
garden.

SA

Outdoor-living area
which can include
table, seating and
barbecue facilities.

OLA

Main paths within
the garden.

Access tracks or
secondary paths.

The number of the
picture described in
the notes following
the plan.

9

Backyard pictures

Picture 1

TREE: *Lagerstroemia speciosa* (Queen's crepe myrtle)

BACKGROUND SHRUBS: *Iochroma tubulosa*

PENINSULA: *Ruellia macrantha*

GROUND PLANTS: *Hypoestes phyllosfachya* 'Splash' (freckleface)

PICTURE: in summer the outdoor living area comes alive with the rosy-purple lagerstroemia and the deep purple iochroma in the background, illuminated by the pink foliage of the carpet of freckleface.

SECONDARY: in winter the ruellias produce their rosy-purple blooms, offset by the pretty hypoestes foliage, which remains attractive throughout the year if kept compact by an occasional trim.

Picture 2

TREE: *Cassia javanica* (java shower)

BACKGROUND SHRUBS: *Bauhinia blakeana*

GROUND PLANTS: *Begonia scharfii*

PICTURE: the early summer flush of huge burgundy-red blooms on the bauhinia provides a strong but beautiful contrast for the light pink cassia above and the pale pink begonias in the foreground.

SECONDARY: the autumn-winter flowering season of the bauhinia creates a rather sinister effect, for at this time the long black pods of the cassia are its companions.

Picture 3

TREE: *Jacaranda acutifolia*

PENINSULA: *Adenandra uniflora, Spiraea cantoniensis*

GROUND PLANTS: *Tulbaghia violacea* 'Tricolor', *Crinum* spp. (white only)

PICTURE: the famous blue-lilac jacaranda blooms are charming with the white of the spiraea and crinums, and the white-streaked purple blooms of the adenandra. The pale violet tulbaghia flowers provide a good finishing touch.

SECONDARY: the tulbaghias continue to produce their tricolour effect of violet, bluish-green and cream until winter weather arrives.

Picture 4

TREE: *Bauhinia variegata* 'Candida'

BACKGROUND SHRUBS: *Hypericum patulum* 'Henryi'

PENINSULA: *Adenandra fragrans*

GROUND PLANTS: *Lobelia laxiflora*

PICTURE: a pretty rosy-pink and white picture is produced in early spring by the adenandras and the bauhinias.

SECONDARY: in summer the scene changes as the hypericums smother themselves with yellow flowers and the lobelias send up their spikes of red and yellow blooms.

Picture 5

TREE: *Ginkgo biloba* (maidenhair tree)

BACKGROUND SHRUBS: *Duranta repens* (*D. plumieri*) (sky flower)

PENINSULAS: *Cordyline terminalis* 'Imperialis', *C.t.* 'Shepherdii'

FOREGROUND SHRUBS: *Jacobinia pauciflora*

GROUND PLANTS: *Reinwardtia indica*

PICTURE: the main display in this section of garden is in the winter when the yellow-orange berries stand out on the durantas, the jacobinias in the foreground produce their red and yellow flowers and the space in between is smothered with yellow reinwardtia blooms. The cordylines at each end with their striking foliage of pink and cream or bronze and green unite to complete a satisfying grouping.

SECONDARY: the durantas produce their lovely blue flowers throughout autumn and into the winter, in some areas highlighted in autumn by the golden leaves of the ginkgo. However, as Brisbane is the northern limit for the growing of this tree, it will sometimes produce its glorious colour as early as February.

Backyard of plan 5

KEY

Deciduous tree
showing expected
ultimate spread.

Deciduous shrub
showing expected
ultimate spread.

Evergreen shrub or
tree showing
expected ultimate
spread.

Peninsula or group of
shrubs.

Climbing plants on
fences, walls or
trellis.

Service area which
can include garden
shed, clothes-line,
compost and rubbish
bins and vegetable
garden.

SA

Outdoor-living area
which can include
table, seating and
barbecue facilities.

OLA

Main paths within
the garden.

Access tracks or
secondary paths.

The number of the
picture described in
the notes following
the plan.

9

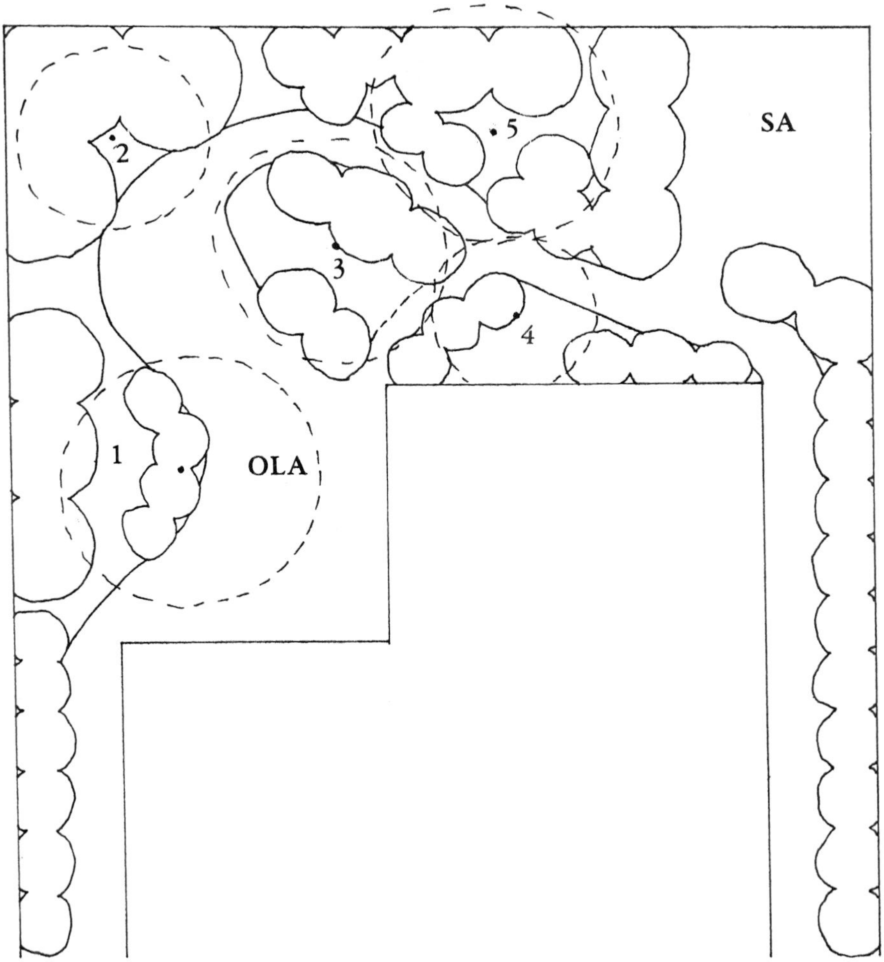

PLAN 6

To suit areas with cool to cold winters and hot and dry summers, such as Perth and many inland urban centres. This garden design shows heavy screening as protection from the hot east and north-east winds which prevail in Perth during summer.

Gardeners with frost-free conditions in Perth will be able to include many plants which are not suitable for inland gardens, but even in these inland areas the larger, hardy trees and shrubs will provide frost protection allowing a wider variety of smaller plants to be used.

Front yard pictures

Picture 1

TREES: *Prunus* x *amygdalo-persica* 'Pollardii', *Robinia pseudoacacia* 'Frisia' (golden robinia) (one only between the prunuses)

BACKGROUND SHRUBS: *Dodonaea viscosa* 'Purpurea' (purple hopbush)

GROUND PLANTS: *Mahonia aquifolium* (oregon grape)

PICTURE: in mid-winter the large, rich-pink prunus blossom is striking against the bronze-purple foliage of the hopbushes.

SECONDARY: the robinia, reputedly non-suckering and spineless, bears long, drooping racemes of white, perfumed flowers in spring, and the lovely fern-like foliage changes from yellow to lime-green, highlighted by the dark backdrop of the hopbushes. The mahonia is interesting all year; the attractive leaves turn bronze and red in the winter and the late-winter and spring blooms of long, yellow trusses are replaced by purplish-black berries.

Picture 2

TREES: *Tamarix pentandra* (late tamarisk)

PENINSULA: *Gossypium sturtianum* (Sturt's desert rose)

GROUND PLANTS: *Iris unguicularis* (*I. stylosa*) (winter iris)

PICTURE: the gossypiums begin producing their large, hibiscus-like bloom in spring, joined in summer by the plumes of the tamarisks. Together they create a delightful rose-pink picture.

SECONDARY: all winter while the tamarisks are bare the iris prolifically provides its sweet-scented lavender flowers.

Picture 3

TREES: *Cercis siliquastrum* (Judas tree), *C.s.* 'Alba' (one only, in the centre)

BACKGROUND SHRUBS: *Hibiscus hueglii*

PENINSULA: *Limonium latifolium* (sea lavender)

GROUND PLANTS: *Iris japonica* (in the densest shade), *Hemiandra pungens* (snake bush)

PICTURE: in early spring the cercis cover themselves, branches and all, with rosy-lilac or white blossom. This striking display is softened by the greyish foliage of the hibiscuses and the first pale lilac flowers of the irises.

SECONDARY: in summer this area presents a symphony of violet-blue as the hibiscuses, limoniums and hemiandras flower in unison for many months.

Picture 4

TREE: *Cedrela sinensis* (Chinese cedar)

SHRUBS: *Teucrium fruticans* (bush germander)

GROUND PLANTS: *Brunonia australis* (blue pincushion)

PICTURE: an unusual colour-scheme is derived in spring from the glossy, pink young foliage of the cedrela and the woolly grey foliage of the teucriums.

SECONDARY: later in the season the deep blue brunonia pincushions and the clusters of pale blue teucrium flowers are charmingly set-off by the foliage of the latter.

Picture 5

TREE: *Fraxinus oxycarpa* 'Raywoodii' (claret ash)

BACKGROUND SHRUBS: *Viburnum tinus*

Front yard of plan 6

KEY

Deciduous tree showing expected ultimate spread.

Deciduous shrub showing expected ultimate spread.

Evergreen shrub or tree showing expected ultimate spread.

Peninsula or group of shrubs.

Climbing plants on fences, walls or trellis.

Service area which can include garden shed, clothes-line, compost and rubbish bins and vegetable garden.

SA

Outdoor-living area which can include table, seating and barbecue facilities.

OLA

Main paths within the garden.

Access tracks or secondary paths.

The number of the picture described in the notes following the plan.

9

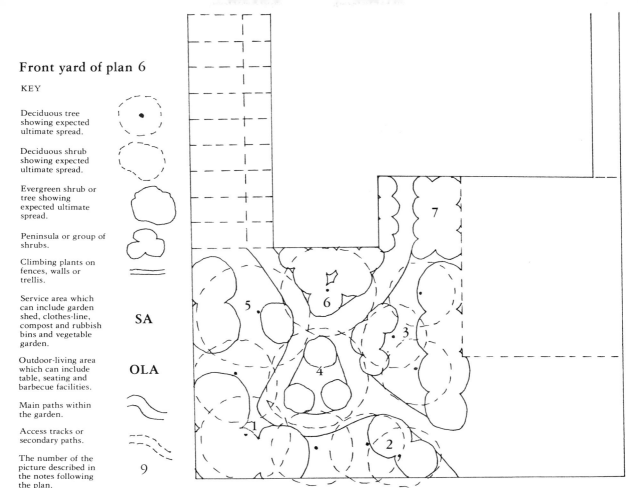

PENINSULA:	*Chaenomeles speciosa* 'Moerloosei' (japonica)
GROUND PLANTS:	*Nerine bowdenii* (pink nerine), *Erigeron karvinskianus* (*E. mucronatus*)
PICTURE:	this is a pretty pink and white setting in early spring, for the chaenomeles has flowers of both colours, enhanced by the white flowers and deep pink buds of the viburnums.
SECONDARY:	for eight months the erigeron produces an abundance of small, white daisies which become pink as they age. In autumn the deep pink nerines are lovely beneath the rich, ruby foliage of the claret ash.

Picture 6

TREE:	*Gleditsia triacanthos* var. *inermis* (honey locust)
BACKGROUND SHRUBS:	*Chrysanthemum frutescens* (marguerite) in lemon or yellow
PENINSULA:	*Chorizema cordatum* (heart-leaf flame pea)
PICTURE:	during winter and spring the chorizemas are massed with their red and yellow flowers, enhanced by the marguerites in winter and enlivened by the fresh green foliage of the gleditsia in spring.

Picture 7

BACKGROUND SHRUBS:	*Santolina chamaecyparissus* (lavender cotton)
FOREGROUND SHRUBS:	*Lechenaultia biloba*
PICTURE:	in winter and spring the pure, deep-blue flowers of the lechenaultias are beautifully highlighted by the silvery-white foliage of the santolinas; one of the most stunning contrasts that a garden can provide.
SECONDARY:	in summer the santolinas have many heads of yellow flowers which are lovely with the white foliage, although some gardeners prefer to remove the flowers to retain the dense white effect.

Backyard pictures

Picture 1

TREES: *Prunus persica* (flowering peach) in a pale-pink, mid-season form
SHRUBS: *Clianthus punicea* (glory pea)
GROUND PLANTS: *Ptilotus exaltatus* (mulla mulla), *Tritonia lineata* var. *rosea*
PICTURE: a delightful soft-pink spring picture of blossom above the haze of woolly, pink ptilotus punctuated by the spikes of delicately-pencilled tritonia blooms
SECONDARY: in early summer the bunches of large red clianthus blooms set among the fern-like foliage are very impressive.

Picture 2

TREES: *Koelreuteria paniculata* (golden rain tree) with the lower branches removed
PENINSULA: *Romneya coulteri* (tree poppy)
BACKGROUND SHRUBS: *Jasminum fruticans* (yellow jasmine), *Eleagnus pungens* 'Maculata' in the centre
FOREGROUND SHRUBS: *Hibbertia montana* var. *major* (mountain primrose). *Santolina charmaecyparissus* (lavender cotton) in between the hibbertias
GROUND PLANTS: *Sternbergia lutea* (lily-of-the-field) as a border in front of the romneyas, *Hibbertia stellaris* and *Anthemis cupaniana* as a ground cover, *Dicleptera suberecta* (orange justica) (one or two plants only)
PICTURE: a progressive picture of silver and gold throughout the year, broken by touches of white, orange and, of course, green foliage. The silver is achieved with the foliage of the romneyas, dicleptesas, anthemis and santolina. Gold is provided by the koelreuteria flowers and autumn foliage, the eleagnus foliage, the centres of the large romneya blooms, and the flowers of the jasmines, hibbertias, santolinas and sternbergias. The touches of orange come from the dicleptera blooms and the mature seed pods of the koelreuterias. The touches of white come from the romneya and anthemis flowers. (To give the sternbergias space in which to bloom, the romneyas are cut down each year in early autumn filling the space again when the sternbergias become dormant in spring.)

Picture 3

BACKGROUND TREES: *Cupressus glabra* 'Hodginsii' or *C.g.* 'Pyramidalis' (upright arizona cypress) (1·2 metres apart)
FOREGROUND SHRUBS: *Cistus* x *cyprius* (rock rose)
PICTURE: even dense wind-breaks can be picture-planned, as is this section. In early summer the abundant white-blotched-red cistus flowers are lovely with a background of the silvery-grey cypress foliage.

Picture 4

BACKGROUND TREES: *Pittosporum crassifolium* 'Variegatum' (variegated karo) 1·2 metres apart
FOREGROUND SHRUBS: *Berberis prattii* (coral barberry)
PICTURE: another section of the wind-break which is beautiful from spring until autumn. The large panicles of yellow berberis flowers, and later the heavy crop of coral-red berries are highlighted by the attractive foliage of the pittosporums.

Picture 5

TREES: *Prunus spinosa* 'Purpurea' (purple-leaf blackthorn), *Gleditsia triacanthos* 'Sunburst' (in the centre)
BACKGROUND SHRUBS:
GROUND PLANTS: *Buddleia salvifolia* (winter buddleia), *Cantua buxifolia* (flower of the Incas) *Oenothera biennis* (biennial evening primrose)
PICTURE: in later winter and early spring the smoky-lilac buddleia plumes are beautiful with the dainty white blossom and young purple leaves of the prunuses.
SECONDARY: a lovely foliage effect is created by the purple leaves of the prunuses combined with the golden, and later lime-green, fern-like leaves of the gleditsia, brightened in spring by the rosy-red blooms of the cantuas, and in summer and autumn by the golden flowers of the oenotheras.

Back yard of plan 6

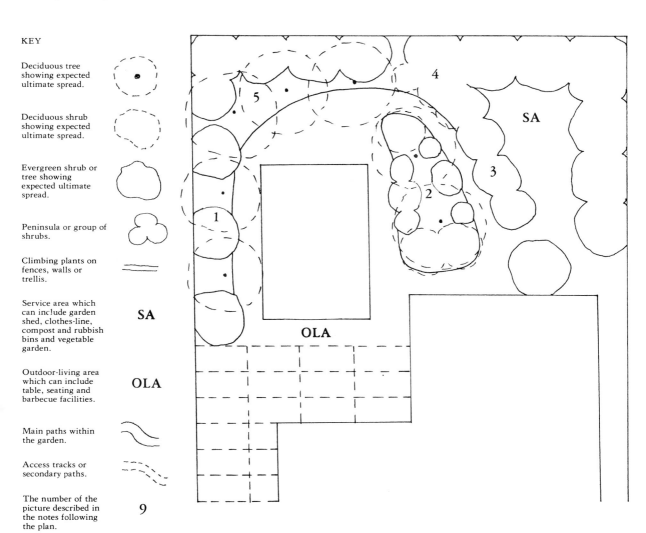

KEY

Deciduous tree
showing expected
ultimate spread.

Deciduous shrub
showing expected
ultimate spread.

Evergreen shrub or
tree showing
expected ultimate
spread.

Peninsula or group of
shrubs.

Climbing plants on
fences, walls or
trellis.

Service area which
can include garden
shed, clothes-line,
compost and rubbish
bins and vegetable
garden.

SA

Outdoor-living area
which can include
table, seating and
barbecue facilities.

OLA

Main paths within
the garden.

Access tracks or
secondary paths.

The number of the
picture described in
the notes following
the plan.

9

PLAN 7

Front yard pictures

To suit gardens with harsh seaside conditions in cool and temperate regions such as the south-east coastline of Australia. When the densely-planted salt-resistant trees and shrubs are well established, less hardy small plants may be placed under their protection.

Picture 1

BACKGROUND TREES: *Acmena cyanocarpo (Eugenia c.)* (blue lilly pilly)
FOREGROUND SHRUBS: *Carissa spectabilis (Acokanthera s.)*
GROUND PLANTS: *Liriope muscari* (blue turf lily)
PICTURE: the violet-blue acmena berries team well in autumn with the purple-black ones of the carissa and the blue-purple spikes of the liriopes, all softened by the neighbouring leucadendron.
SECONDARY: in early summer the carissa and the acmenas produce abundant white blooms, and in winter the leaves of the carissa become deep purple.

Picture 2

TREES: *Prunus cerasifera* 'Nigra' (purple-leaf cherry plum)
BACKGROUND TREES: *Leucadendron argenteum* (silver tree)
PENINSULA: *Protea grandiceps* 'Susannae'
GROUND PLANTS: *Bergenia cordifolia* 'Purpurea'
PICTURE: the large heads of mauve-pink bergenia blooms light up the winter garden and are joined in early spring by the pretty pink blossom and dark purple leaves of the prunuses, lovely with the shimmering silvery backdrop of the leucadendrons.

Picture 3

TREES: *Tamarix pentandra* (late tamarisk)
BACKGROUND SHRUBS: *Buddleia davidii* 'Royal Red'
GROUND PLANTS: *Salvia* x *superba* 'Lubeck'
PICTURE: in summer the stunning red-purple racemes of the buddleias and salvias are softened by the rose-pink plumes and glaucous foliage of the tamarisks.

Picture 4

TREE: *Paulownia tomentosa* (royal paulownia)
BACKGROUND TREES: *Myoporum laetum*
FOREGROUND SHRUBS: *Westringia fruticosa* (coast rosemary)
PICTURE: the fragrant spikes of blue-purple flowers on the paulownia are nicely complemented in spring by the blooms of the myoporums and westringias, which are white speckled with purple.

Picture 5

TREES: *Cratageus phaenopyrum* (Washington thorn)
PENINSULA: *Sparmannia africana*
ACCENT SHRUBS: *Yucca filamentosa*
GROUND PLANTS: *Hedera canariensis* 'Variegata' (kept as a ground cover)
PICTURE: in spring the large, white snowballs of the sparmannia and the white crataegus flowers are lovely above the green and cream carpet of the ivy.
SECONDARY: in summer the ivory-white spires of yucca bells are charming above this pretty carpet, as is the autumn display of red crataegus foliage and berries.

Front yard of plan 7

KEY

Deciduous tree showing expected ultimate spread.

Deciduous shrub showing expected ultimate spread.

Evergreen shrub or tree showing expected ultimate spread.

Peninsula or group of shrubs.

Climbing plants on fences, walls or trellis.

Service area which can include garden shed, clothes-line, compost and rubbish bins and vegetable garden.

SA

Outdoor-living area which can include table, seating and barbecue facilities.

OLA

Main paths within the garden.

Access tracks or secondary paths.

The number of the picture described in the notes following the plan.

9

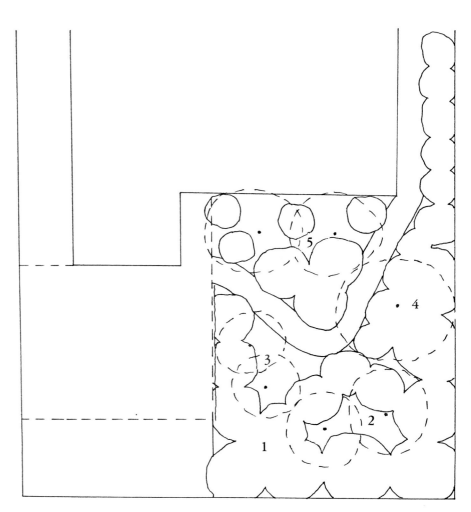

Backyard pictures

Picture 1

TREE: *Koelreuteria paniculata* (golden rain tree) with the lower branches removed
BACKGROUND SHRUB: *Aucuba japonica* 'Gold Dust' (gold dust laurel)
PENINSULA: *Choisya ternata* (Mexican orange blossom)
GROUND PLANTS: *Fuchsia procumbens*
PICTURE: the large panicles of koelreuteria flowers brighten this corner in summer, set off nicely by the large, gold-speckled aucuba leaves and the glossy green foliage of the choisyas. The small but attractive fuchsia flowers provide a carpet of yellowish-green and orange with touches of purple.
SECONDARY: in late spring and early summer the choisyas produce their white, sweet-scented blooms in abundance. The foliage of the aucuba and the choisyas provide an attractive contrast all year.

Picture 2

TREES: *Prunus* x *blireiana* (double-rose cherry plum) with the lower branches removed
BACKGROUND SHRUBS: *Viburnum tinus*
SHRUBS: *Hydrangea villosa*
PENINSULA: *Echium virescens* (*E. candicans*) (pride of Madiera)
GROUND PLANTS: *Salvia farinacea* (mealy-cup sage)
PICTURE: in late spring and summer the striking spikes of echium blooms, which are actually blue with pink stamens, appear to radiate a violet haze, echoed by the salvias and hydrangeas (although the latter will be pinker in alkaline soils). The red-purple summer foliage of the prunuses is particularly handsome in this violet setting.
SECONDARY: the abundant pink blossom nestled among the dark burgundy young leaves of the prunuses is charming with the early spring blooms of the viburnums, opening white from burgundy buds.

Picture 3

TREES: *Tamarix parviflora* (early tamarisk), *Cercis siliquastrum* (Judas tree)
PENINSULAS: *Leycesteria formosa* (Himalayan honeysuckle), *Fuchsia magellanica* (lady's eardrops)
ACCENT PLANTS: *Yucca filamentosa*
GROUND PLANTS: *Pulsatilla vulgaris* (pasque flower)
PICTURE: in spring the rosy-lilac flowers of the cercis appear in clusters on every stem and branch, associating attractively with the feathery plumes of the tamarisk and the chalice-shaped blooms of the pulsatillas. (This is a good time to prune the fuchsias, particularly if their flowers intrude in this picture.)
SECONDARY: in summer the leycesterias bear their small, white flowers peeping out from unusual chains of claret-red bracts which hang daintily above the spires of ivory-white yucca blooms. The dark-red and blue fuchsia flowers combine prettily in this setting.

Picture 4

PENINSULA: *Camellia sasanqua* 'Spencer's Pink'
SHRUBS: *Rosa rugosa* 'Sarah van Fleet', *R.* 'Ballerina'
GROUND PLANTS: *Heuchera* x *brizoides* in a pale pink form, *Limonium dicksonii* (*L. roseum*)
PICTURE: the glossy, dark-green camellia foliage is the perfect backdrop for the lovely, pink, summer display given by the roses and perennials.
SECONDARY: in mid-autumn the camellias begin a prolonged display of pale-pink, perfumed blooms.

Picture 5

TREES: *Lagerstroemia indica* (pink crepe myrtle)
BACKGROUND SHRUBS: *Escallonia* x *fretheyii*
PENINSULA: *Correa reflexa*, *Euphorbia wulfenii* (in between the correas)
GROUND PLANTS: *Phlox paniculata*, mainly white with some pink

Backyard of plan 7

KEY

Deciduous tree
showing expected
ultimate spread.

Deciduous shrub
showing expected
ultimate spread.

Evergreen shrub or
tree showing
expected ultimate
spread.

Peninsula or group of
shrubs.

Climbing plants on
fences, walls or
trellis.

Service area which
can include garden
shed, clothes-line,
compost and rubbish
bins and vegetable
garden.

SA

Outdoor-living area
which can include
table, seating and
barbecue facilities.

OLA

Main paths within
the garden.

Access tracks or
secondary paths.

The number of the
picture described in
the notes following
the plan.

9

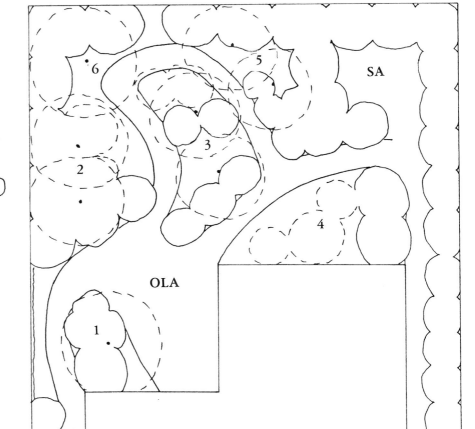

| PICTURE: | a pretty pink and white summer setting is provided by the lagerstroemias, escallonias and phlox. |
| SECONDARY: | the peninsula of this area emerges in winter to display the unusual greenish-yellow bracts of the euphorbia and the blooms of the correas, which are red tipped with purple. |

Picture 6

TREE:	*Gleditsia triacanthos* 'Sunburst' (golden gleditsia)
BACKGROUND SHRUBS:	*Dodonaea viscosa* 'Purpurea' (purple hopbush)
GROUND PLANTS:	*Alchemilla mollis* (lady's mantle)
PICTURE:	from bud-break until leaf-fall this corner features the lovely foliage contrast of the golden gleditsia backed by the bronze-purple dodonaeas.
SECONDARY:	when the gleditsia foliage turns in summer to fresh, lime-green, the alchemilla becomes a froth of greenish-yellow beneath it.

INDEX